FISKE

250

words every high school freshman needs to know

SECOND EDITION

FISKE

250

words every high school freshman needs to know

SECOND EDITION

EDWARD B. FISKE
JANE MALLISON AND DAVID HATCHER

sourcebooks

Published by Sourcebooks, Inc.
P.O. Box 4410, Naperville, Illinois 60567-4410
(630) 961-3900
Fax: (630) 961-2168
www.sourcebooks.com

The Library of Congress has catalogued the first edition as follows:

Fiske, Edward B.
  Fiske 250 words every high school freshman needs to know / by Edward B. Fiske, Jane Mallison, and David Hatcher.
      p. cm.
  1. Vocabulary. 2. High school freshmen—Language. I. Mallison, Jane. II. Hatcher, David. III. Title. IV. Title: Fiske two-hundred fifty words every high school freshman needs to know.
  PE1449.F5528 2009
  428.1—dc22

                              2008048508

Printed and bound in the United States of America.
            VP 10 9 8 7 6 5 4 3 2 1

contents

introduction

Chances are that you already know lots of words—probably tens of thousands. And now you are about to learn even more.

Not that we blame you—obviously, we're glad you're enlarging your hoard of words. You can probably already reel off some excellent reasons for learning more words: people with rich vocabularies make higher grades, score better on most standardized tests, and go on to be more successful in their chosen careers. They're also more interesting to talk to.

All these are valid reasons for expanding and refining your vocabulary. We'd like to add a couple more that we find equally valid.

One is that learning new words actually makes you smarter. You don't just seem smarter, you are smarter—you know more. Oliver Wendell Holmes, Jr., was right when he said a mind stretched by a new idea never goes back to its original dimensions. What's true for ideas is true for words. When you learn the word symbiosis, you become linked to the knowledge that plants and animals have worked out some fascinating and mutually beneficial ways to help each other—from the bird that cleans food fragments from the alligator's teeth to the tiny mite that clings to the bottom of an ant's foot (getting a bit of food from the ant's system, and perhaps serving as an athletic shoe to cushion the host's soles).

But getting smarter through learning words isn't limited to the acquisition of technical terms. As a friend once said, "If you know the names of the wildflowers, you're more likely to see them." That principle works for words as well. Once you learn the adjective *louche*, for example, you'll be able to recognize, to pinpoint, a variety of decadent slyness that you might earlier have tossed in the catchall basket labeled *weird*.

Here's one more reason, often overlooked but for us among the most important—you can learn words for the pure pleasure of it, for the joy of discovery, of finding out what the words mean, how they sound, maybe when they were born, where they come from, and how they've changed over the years. (Did you know a *bonfire* was once a *bone fire*?)

Isn't it a pleasure to know that there's a word for the pesky person who delights in catching others' errors—and triumphantly pointing them out? That person's a *doryphore* (DORY-for). Or what about the fact that *crapulous* describes someone with a hangover?

And you doubtless know someone who talks too much—way too much. The person who goes on and on, sending out a seemingly unending flow of words, is suffering (or making us suffer) from *logorrhea* (LOG-uh-REE-uh).

So you have lots of reasons for expanding and deepening your vocabulary, and the words we've chosen for this book run the gamut. We think they'll help you satisfy all your reasons for learning new words, and that you'll find them interesting, useful, and fun.

Feel free to dive into this book anywhere you like, but if you start at the beginning, you'll recognize a pattern of four chapters organized by themes, followed by a grab bag chapter, and a quiz over five chapters. If you complete the entire book (congratulations!), you'll have encountered two hundred words in the thematic chapters, learned fifty from the grab bag chapters, and taken five quizzes to reinforce your confidence that you've mastered them all.

This book follows the style and format of its parent book, *Fiske WordPower*, which contains one thousand words.* So when you're ready for lots more, move on to *Fiske WordPower*, by Edward B. Fiske, Jane Mallison, and Margery Mandell (Sourcebooks, 2006). You'll find hundreds of new words there—some practical, some intriguing, some both—and you'll recognize a few familiar friends you first met here.

---

* We've also written a sibling book, *Fiske 250 Words Every High School Graduate Needs to Know*, with a set of slightly more challenging words that are completely different from those in the book you're holding now—take a look.

1 animal words

Rightly or wrongly, we ascribe certain qualities to animals—the loyalty of dogs, the independence of cats, the bravery of lions. And we use those associations to help us describe people and things. If you mention a dancer's feline grace, you give your listeners an instant image that helps get your message across. The following words—not as common as feline or canine—can be a great help when you want to describe other people and their attitudes.

1. Leonine (LEO-nine)

Picture someone with erect posture, a flowing mane of hair, and feline, fluid movements. Leonine, or "lionlike," would be a good descriptive adjective. It can describe behavior, appearance, or both.

- *The senator stood straight and tall, his handsome gray hair swaying as he gestured grandly—a* **leonine** *presence among lamblike listeners.*

- *Weaving gracefully and rapidly among the other players, Lee gave an absolutely* **leonine** *performance.*

2. Vulpine (VUL-pin or VUL-pine)

Literally meaning "like a fox," this term can help you describe anyone or anything that resembles the animal—in looks, attitude, or action. A female fox is technically called a **vixen**, and that term is also used figuratively for a human female who can cause trouble.

- *The poker player's long nose and pointed ears gave him a **vulpine** appearance that matched his crafty play.*

- *"She was a **vixen** when she went to school," complained Shakespeare's Helena in a temporary spat with her good friend Hermia.*

3. Ursine (UR-sine)

Ursa means "bear," so this adjective means "bearlike." It's used primarily to describe physical size or shape, but can suggest a style of dress or behavior as well.

- *The watchman was an **ursine** man, husky and shambling, with a curly beard and thick head of hair.*

- *I can't be sure it was actually a bear I saw, but it definitely had an **ursine** shape.*

4. Equine (EE-kwine or EK-wine)

This adjective describes anything bearing the characteristics of animals such as horses, asses, or zebras. **Equestrian**, on the other hand, is an adjective that describes anything having to do with horseback riding. (An equestrian is also a man who rides horses, while an equestrienne is a female horseback rider.)

- *Equine* studies is a branch of the veterinary field that involves the care and treatment of horses and related animals.

- This store specializes in **equestrian** products such as saddles, reins, bits, and blankets.

5. Bovine (BO-vine)

This adjective means "of or relating to the characteristics of cows, oxen, or buffaloes." It also means "sluggish and dull"—like the behavior of most cows.

- *The veterinarian specialized in **bovine** diseases because most of the families in the area were dairy farmers.*

- *With a **bovine** expression on his face, the child stared blankly at the television screen and munched on a cookie.*

"She was a **vixen** when she went to school," complained Shakespeare's Helena in a temporary spat with her good friend Hermia.

6. Reptilian (rep-TILL-ee-un)

Rarely used in a complimentary manner (by anyone other than herpetologists), this word means just what it suggests—"in some way resembling a snake, lizard, crocodile, or other such creeping creature." The word comes from a Latin term for "creeping."

- *The prisoner was intimidated by the cold manner and* **reptilian** *eyes of the interrogator.*

- *Many* **reptilian** *animals may appear sluggish, but can move with frightening alacrity when attacking.*

7. Avian (AY-vee-an)

This adjective means "having the characteristics of birds." An **aviary**, on the other hand, is a large structure for holding birds in confinement.

- *The* **avian** *Michael Jordan took off from the foul line, flying to the basket for a dunk.*

- *There is an* **aviary** *at the zoo that contains brilliantly colored parrots, toucans, and peacocks.*

8. Simian (SIM-ee-an)

Anyone who resembles an ape or a monkey might be described by the adjective *simian*.

- *With* **simian** *intensity, the mother sat before her child and carefully picked the leaves and sticks from his hair.*

- *The lead actor in* The Hairy Ape *had near-perfect* **simian** *expressions and movements.*

9. Porcine (POUR-sine)

This adjective means "resembling a swine or a pig," either in appearance or behavior. The sentences below reveal both meanings.

- *Stuffing an assortment of meats and cheeses into his* **porcine** *face, the obese man smiled contentedly at the buffet table and contemplated going back for more.*

- *He collected **porcine** objects—such as piggy banks and Porky the Pig comic books.*

10. Anthropoid (ANN-thruh-poid)

Well, fair's fair, so let's end this list with a look in the mirror. Just as we compare humans to animals, we sometimes compare animals (and other things, like robots) to humans. This word comes from the Greek term for "mankind."

- *The **anthropoid** apes may have given rise to many of the reported sightings of Bigfoot and other feral, half-human mythical creatures of folklore.*

- *C-3PO had a more **anthropoid** appearance than his friend R2-D2.*

2 words ending in -*ate*

That *ate* on the end of a word isn't a sure sign that you're dealing with a verb—although most of the words that follow are verbs. It can also be a suffix on an adjective, noun, or other part of speech.

1. Exacerbate (ex-ASS-er-bate)

When you exacerbate something, you aggravate it or increase its severity. Its Latin root means "to make harsh." The noun form is **exacerbation**.

- *The swelling in Mrs. Cunningham's knee was **exacerbated** by the fact that she had to keep bending down to pick up the toys left on the floor by her twin sons, Aiden and Frank.*

- *The antics of disc jockeys like DJ Hamentashen **exacerbate** the pop music industry's image as contrived, superficial, and manic.*

2. Pixilate (PIX-ul-ate)

We're taking a little poetic license here, because the word almost always has a *d* on the end. You'd use it to describe someone who's a little wacky, eccentric, or whimsically prankish. It comes from the idea that pixies could jumble up someone's thinking.

- *Lyn's not quite certifiably crazy, just a little **pixilated**.*

- *Those kids are driving the teacher to distraction— they're absolutely **pixilating** her.*

3. Obviate (OB-vee-ate)

To obviate is to make something unnecessary, no longer needed.

- *This sudden rain **obviates** the need to water the garden.*

- *To **obviate** the danger of electrocution, you should cut off the power before changing the switch.*

4. Placate (PLAY-kate)

There seem to be plenty of verbs that mean "to lessen someone's anger or hard feelings," and here's another one. One placates under the same conditions that one mollifies.

- *A man of integrity, William made a point of never **placating** his enemies with lies or empty promises.*

- *Almost any political office involves a fair amount of groveling and manipulating in order to **placate** a constituency with a broad range of demands and needs.*

5. Titillate (TIT-ill-ate)

You can use this word to describe physical or emotional feelings. In either case, it means "to excite or arouse pleasurably."

- *The music is **titillating**—it makes you want to dance with someone.*

- *The hikers sat under the waterfall, laughing as the cool water **titillated** their sun-baked skin.*

*Those kids are driving the teacher to distraction—they're absolutely **pixilating** her.*

6. Remonstrate (ri-MON-strate)

When you voice strong objection or disapproval, you are remonstrating.

- *She scolded the boy for his inattention, but her **remonstrations** had little effect.*

- *We should **remonstrate** when our so-called public servants violate their promises and our trust.*

7. Interpolate (in-TUR-po-late)

As the prefix *inter-* (meaning "between") suggests, this word means "to put something between other things." This may be done for good reasons (as to make something clear), or for the purpose of deception.

- *"What he means," she **interpolated**, "is that the animal is a crocodile."*

- *The excellent editor's **interpolations** helped make the dense prose clear.*

8. Perambulate (per-AM-byu-late)

Here's a fancy verb for "to walk" or "to stroll." It can also mean "to walk through" as in "to inspect on foot." It comes from the Latin for "walk" and "through." The British have found another use for it. They call a baby carriage a **perambulator**.

- *After the company picnic, the park service staff **perambulated** the grounds, making sure there were no lost or left items and no damage done to park property.*

- *Every evening after a light supper, Mr. Bartleby takes a constitutional, during which he **perambulates** the streets along the waterfront and watches the ships unload their cargo.*

9. Vacillate (VASS-ill-ate)

A good verb for talking about change, it means "to swing indecisively from one idea or action to another." The noun form is **vacillation**.

- *Casey **vacillated** between going to school with a cold (because she had a math test) and staying home and getting some rest.*

- *After work, the busy mother **vacillated** between ordering in Chinese food and cooking a simple chicken dinner.*

10. Abnegate (AB-nig-ate)

This word is often used with *self*, because it means "to deny oneself something"—as in rights, comforts, or privileges.

- *The priest was proud of his **self-abnegation** of all things luxurious.*

- *Ella wasn't about to **abnegate** her right to speak at the council meeting.*

3 words for change

The only constant, it's been said, is change. We're always concerned about change. If things are good, we hope they won't change; if they're bad, we hope they will. And we listen to (and often elect) those who promise to bring it about. Things change in many ways—for better, or for worse. The following words are useful in describing some of the ways that happens.

1. Diaspora (dye-ASS-por-ah)

This noun comes to us from the Greek word for "dispersion" or "scattering." With a capital *D,* it refers to the dispersion of the Jews from the time (sixth century BC) of their exile to Babylonia. It may also be used to refer to any such dispersion—of a people, language, or culture.

- *The violence and persecution of the Jews during World War II continued the **Diaspora** that led many Jews to settle not only in the United States but in Latin America as well.*

- *There was a great **diaspora** of Europeans to New York's Lower East Side at the turn of the twentieth century; Italian, Polish, and Irish immigrants arrived in droves to seek opportunities for a better life.*

2. Disseminate (dis-EM-in-ate)

This verb comes from the Latin for "to sow." It means "to scatter widely" or "to disperse," as in sowing seed.

- *In her work* My Fight for Birth Control, *Margaret Sanger describes her struggle to provide birth control information, which was illegal to **disseminate** in the early part of the twentieth century.*

- *In order to discourage cigarette smoking, the American Cancer Society **disseminates** information on lung cancer and heart disease on its website and through printed pamphlets distributed in doctors' offices throughout the country.*

3. Harbinger (HAR-bin-jer)

This noun refers to a forerunner, an early warning or messenger of what's to come. Its interesting origin derives from a person sent ahead to provide lodging for one to come. (If you've traveled in Francophone Canada or France, you may hear a hint of this word in their term *auberge,* or inn.)

- *The robin is famous as a **harbinger** of spring, no matter what the calendar might say.*

- *Getting an A on his first paper in anthropology class was a **harbinger** of the fact that he would win the Margaret Mead Prize at the end of the year.*

4. **Ephemeral** (ee-FEM-er-al)

This adjective comes from the Greek word that means "day" and, though it originally meant "lasting only a day," it now describes anything short-lived or fleeting. The noun form **ephemera** refers to printed matter—such as newspapers, greeting cards, or calling cards—that have relevance or hold interest for only a passing amount of time.

- *The Peruvian novelist Mario Vargas Llosa once said, "No matter how **ephemeral** it is, a novel is something, while despair is nothing."*

- *At the antiques fair on the pier, we visited the stall of a dealer who specializes in **ephemera**, including old maps, nineteenth-century women's magazines, Victorian postcards, and daguerreotypes.*

5. **Epiphany** (ee-PIF-uh-nee)

This noun refers to any instant perception, sudden comprehension, or spontaneous revelation. A cartoonist might indicate the epiphany of a character by drawing a lightbulb over his head. The root word in Greek means "to show." When capitalized, the word has the specific meaning of a Christian holiday observed on January 6, when, as tradition expresses it, the Magi or Three Kings arrived in Bethlehem to see the newborn Jesus.

- *Tiffany asked me if her realization that Chip just wasn't that interested in her could count as an **epiphany** like those in the stories of James Joyce.*

- *The secular concept of the Twelve Days of Christmas has its origins in the religious holiday of **Epiphany**.*

*The Peruvian novelist Mario Vargas
Llosa once said, "No matter how
ephemeral it is,
a novel is something, while
despair is nothing."*

6. Messianic (MES-ee-AN-ik)

Literally, this adjective refers to a Messiah, a figure in
the Judeo-Christian tradition that is or will be a savior
of the world. By extension, it's often used to refer to
zealous or overzealous belief in a cause or a leader. The
word comes from the Hebrew for "anointed."

- *"There's nothing wrong with green algae," noted
  Don, "but when Doug starts talking about it he gets
  that **messianic** gleam in his eye as if taking algae
  could cure all the ills of the world."*

- *Some earlier interpreters of Virgil saw a **messianic**
  theme in one of his early poems, but skeptics argue
  he was merely flattering a Roman leader, suggesting
  that his child would be remarkable.*

7. Posthumous (PAHS-tyoo-mus)

Literally meaning "after death," this adjective has a
special "family sense" in referring to a baby born after
the death of his or her father. It can also be used in
nonfamily contexts.

- *Modern-day psychologists have written about the
  childhood of eighteenth-century writer Jonathan Swift:*

*not only was he a **posthumous** child, but his mother was geographically distant from him in his early years.*

- *Sicilian writer Giuseppe Lampedusa's only novel, The Leopard, was published **posthumously** to great acclaim; the writer knew only the sadness of having his manuscript rejected twice.*

8. Junta (HOON-ta)

This Spanish word for a "small group" has come into English; it denotes either a small group of military officers seizing power in a country or a small legislative body, usually in Central or South America.

- *Though not quite a **junta**, Lee's old prep-school ties with Greg and Eddie have been strong enough to switch some votes in their college fraternity.*

- *Some erudite readers can recall the multilingual New Yorker cartoon of some years past that depicts a small group of men entering a corporate office, saying, "We're a **junta** and this is a coup."*

9. Galvanize (GAL-va-nize)

This verb originally had the literal meaning of "shocking someone with an electric current." Today, it carries only the figurative meaning of "spurring someone into thought or action." The existence of the word bears permanent tribute to Luigi Galvani, an eighteenth-century doctor whose early research stimulated further experiments with electricity.

- *The school principal used her assembly talk about poverty in this country to **galvanize** her* students into an understanding of the importance of compassion.

- Some groups that once fought for the right to vote are no longer **galvanized** by the importance of using that privilege.

10. Valediction (val-uh-DIK-shun)

A rather formal farewell statement is called a valediction. Most schools still select a **valedictorian**, the student with the highest grades in the class who gets the official right to make a "good-bye speech" at graduation exercises.

- General Douglas MacArthur's **valedictory** speech to Congress in April 1951 is remembered chiefly for his moving quotation from an old barracks ballad: "Old soldiers never die; they just fade away."

- John Keats, knowing of his imminent death from tuberculosis, attempts, with sadness, to write, from Rome, a **valediction** to a friend in England, "I can scarcely bid you goodbye even in a letter. I always made an awkward bow."

4 class words

A democracy attempts to destroy rigid barriers of social class that have characterized older social orders; nonetheless, social class remains a hot topic today. As an example, *elite* can be used as a compliment or a sneer. (It derives from the same word as *elect*, a word for someone or something that's chosen out of the crowd.)

1. Patrician (pa-TRISH-un)

In ancient Rome the patricians were the unashamed aristocrats, those who had access to wealth and to the great majority of positions of rule. The girl's name Patricia is a direct offspring.

- *On his father's side Professor Greene descended from **patrician** stock, ancestors who literally came over on the* Mayflower, *but he identified more with the vitality of his mother's Irish roots.*

- *The playwright A. R. Gurney often deals with mildly **patrician** customs such as the cocktail hour and the placement of salad forks.*

2. Plebeian (pleh-BE-un)

In ancient Rome the plebeians were the complement to the patricians. Today the noun can be used descriptively in that historic sense or contemptuously, in reference to unrefined tastes or preferences. (First-year students at the United States Military Academy are informally known as **plebes**—the lowest order.)

- *While others at the table chose dishes like foie gras and medallions of veal, Lou asked the server if the chef could make him a **plebeian** grilled cheese sandwich.*

- *Shakespeare's play* Julius Caesar *pictures the **plebeians** in the Forum for Caesar's funeral as being easily swayed by Marc Antony's skillful rhetoric.*

3. Hierarchy (HI-er-ark-ee or HIRE-ark-ee)

A hierarchy is a ranking of people or things in order of importance, ability, or status. You'll often hear informal nicknames such as "pecking order" or "totem pole." The fact that the first four letters sound like *higher* is just a coincidence: the word comes from the Greek for "rule by a priest."

- *In the **hierarchy** of jobs, summer photocopying intern was one of the lowest; nonetheless, Brett greatly enjoyed working at the magazine.*

- *"I doubt that the president of the company will answer our complaint," said Joe to Linda. "He'll pass it on to someone lower in the **hierarchy**."*

4. Caste (rhymes with *past*)

A caste is a formal or informal social class or subclass, a concept originating in traditional Hindu society.

- *Aldous Huxley's futurist novel* Brave New World *features a society with five rigidly defined **castes**: Alpha, Beta, Gamma, Delta, and Epsilon.*

- *The insect world is no democracy: ants have a very firm **caste** system, with each insect playing its own special role.*

5. Bourgeois (BOOR-zhwa)

This word is an adjective, neutrally defined as "middle class, probably an owner of property." Often, though, it has a negative connotation, a mocking of a supposed attitude of conformity to accepted standards. Coming into English from French, it's ultimately related to the suffix -burg, meaning "town." The plural noun form is bourgeoisie (BOOR-zhwa-ZEE).

- *The book of local history of Yountville recorded the fact that the town council had to find a resolution between the conflicting needs of the **bourgeoisie** and those of the working class.*

- *Does William really want a question mark shaved into the hair on the back of his head, or is he just trying to shock what he calls the **bourgeois** values of his parents?*

*The playwright A. R. Gurney often deals with mildly **patrician** customs such as the cocktail hour and the placement of salad forks.*

6. Proletarian (prole-a-TARE-ee-un)

This adjective refers to those who do not own property but live by selling their labor—in short, the working class, the **proletariat**. It derives from the Latin word for "offspring," because the children of the working class in ancient Rome were considered the greatest contribution of the workers.

- *Those who work to market the "image" of presidential candidates in the United States sometimes create the odd situation of having a multimillionaire candidate pretending to have **proletarian** tastes in food and recreation.*

- *The documentary film attempted to show both the dark and the bright side of the **proletarian** life: concern about supporting the family, and a feeling of solidarity with neighbors and fellow workers.*

7. Hoi polloi (HOY puh-LOY)

It's Greek for "the masses," "the many." (See how that second word resembles the prefix *poly-* as in *polygon*?) In English it means "common people," or the plural version of "the man in the street." And once it becomes an English phrase, it's used with *the*; only pedants worry about *hoi* meaning "the" in Greek! And don't confuse it with the slang phrase *hoity-toity*, which is a scornful way of referring to someone of an allegedly higher economic status.

- *Eustace found it patronizing that those who attacked the controversial magazine cover worried particularly about its impact on the **hoi polloi**.*

- *For all the intensive work on refining survey techniques, no pundit is willing to predict with certainty what the **hoi polloi** will do once they get inside the voting booth.*

8. Parvenu (PAR-vuh-noo)

A newcomer to a "higher" level of social or economic status, one who doesn't yet know "how it's done"—this French noun brings with it into English a nondemocratic, judgmental perspective.

- *"Hubert, that **parvenu**? I would never trust him to advise me on my finances. He doesn't even know how to place his silver at the end of the meal," Mrs. Hayes sniffily observed.*

- *Although his wealthy guests from the fashionable side of the bay were happy to attend Jay Gatsby's parties and drink his illegal alcohol, they continued to regard him as a **parvenu**, a man with a fancy automobile but without a horse.*

9. Noblesse oblige (no-BLESS o-BLEEZH)

Literally, this phrase of French origin refers to the honorable behavior expected of those born into a higher social class. Today, it must be used with care, for its meaning has changed from a literal statement about class expectations. It now carries an insulting sense of "You think you're better than I am."

- *In eighteenth-century England the continuing tradition of **noblesse oblige** prompted owners of great estates to ensure the lifelong welfare of servants on the estate.*

- *"Tell Lady Sneerwell to forget that **noblesse oblige** stuff," snorted Charles. "I want to be paid a decent wage for myself and my family, not be given a frozen turkey at Christmas!"*

10. Morganatic (mor-gan-AT-ik)

This fascinating adjective from a custom in the medieval period refers to a type of legal marriage between someone of noble or royal birth and a person of lower status. In such a union, both parties agreed that the person of lower rank would not receive the title or all privileges of the higher-ranking partner. (Perhaps there's the built-in sense of a "love match" rather than a politically derived union?)

You may see the similar term *plaçage*, from the French word meaning "to place with." It is sometimes used for marital arrangements, similar to common-law marriages; for example: The emperor not only condoned *plaçage* for his men, he ordered his aides to facilitate it, in order to sustain the morale of the men.

- *When Prince Charles, the Duke of Wales, controversially married Camilla Parker-Bowles, she assumed a title other than the traditional "Duchess of Wales." Was this some holdover from earlier **morganatic** customs?*

- *The heroine of the Mary McCarthy novel felt that her happy second marriage caused neighbors to beam at her and her new mate as if they were **morganatic**.*

5

farrago

This is one of five chapters where you're offered a mixed bag of useful words. The word *farrago* (fuh-RAH-go) itself comes from the Latin for "a medley of grains used for feed," and has come to mean "a mixture." It's a synonym for *gallimaufry*, *hodgepodge*, *olio*, and *potpourri*, words you'll also find in this book.

1. Pique (peek)

This verb comes to us from the French and means "to prick" or "to provoke." It can also be used as a noun to mean "a feeling of wounded pride" or "indignation."

- *"Your description of the restaurant really **piqued** my curiosity. I've never tasted Asian-Lithuanian cuisine before, and it sounds delicious," Patty said, patting her stomach.*

- *In a fit of **pique**, Lotta threw away her scale and said, "I'm tired of trying to look like the skinny models in all the fashion magazines. I'm chubby and I like myself just the way I am!"*

2. Corpulent (KOR-pyu-lent)

From the Latin word meaning "body," this adjective means "having a lot of body" or "excessively fat." Someone who is corpulent is obese. The noun form is **corpulence**.

- *"A high-fat diet is almost guaranteed to cause* **corpulence**," *said Dr. Pritikin. "Stick with fruits and vegetables if you want to stay slim."*

- *Despite his* **corpulence**, *the actor Jackie Gleason was a graceful dancer. He carried himself like a man who was one hundred pounds lighter.*

3. Leery (rhymes with *cheery*)

If you're leery of something or someone, you're suspicious or mistrustful of them. (In current use it's interestingly not related to the word *leer*, which refers to an unwelcome, provocative look.)

- *While I know they're probably just trying to earn a living, I'm very* **leery** *of people who telephone me with special offers and supposedly great bargains.*

- *Uncle Vernon's favorite statement, "There's no free lunch," was designed to remind us to be* **leery** *of anything that looks too easy; "payment" of some kind will eventually be required.*

4. Clandestine (clan-DES-tin)

Probably formed from the Latin for "internal secret," this adjective is used to describe something done secretly in order to conceal a private plan or an improper purpose. People aren't clandestine; actions are.

- *In a **clandestine** meeting that took place in his London war rooms, Winston Churchill met with his cabinet to discuss the impending deployment of British troops.*

- *Knowing their parents would forbid their union, Romeo and Juliet arranged a **clandestine** marriage by Friar Lawrence, who saw in their love the possibility of ending the age-old feud between the Capulets and the Montagues.*

5. Capricious (cah-PRISH-us)

This adjective comes from the Italian for "fright" or "sudden start" and means "unpredictable," "impulsive," or "subject to whim." The noun form is **caprice**.

- ***Capricious** by nature, Samantha was warm to her friends on Monday morning but quite aloof in the afternoon.*

- *Ruled by **caprice**, Professor Mason was sometimes an easy grader and other times quite strict, frustrating his ambitious students and amusing the indolent ones.*

*The fact that there are eighty **extant** manuscripts of Chaucer's poetry from the early fifteenth century testifies to his popularity.*

6. Constituent (kon-STIT-u-ent)

Politically speaking, a constituent is a resident of a region represented by a certain elected official. In a larger sense, it could be any person who is represented by someone else. A group of constituents, or the region where they live, is called a **constituency**.

- *Representative O'Toole made a hasty pre-election flight from Washington to his home state so that he could meet with his **constituents**, learn their concerns, and impress upon them that he needed their votes.*

- *Students who were appointed to committees were told they would be practicing "non-**constituency**-based" stewardship; in short, they'd be giving their own views, not necessarily views held by a majority of the student body.*

7. Waspish (WASP-ish)

This adjective describes a person who's irritable or a remark or attitude that's spiteful. It's only a coincidence that the first syllable is the same as the acronymic nickname for an ethnic/religious group: this equal opportunity word comes directly from the flying insect that can sting—and hurt.

- *When Junior made a slimy joke about his sister's recent weight gain, she stung back at him: "How can anyone of your age and intelligence be so **waspish**?"*

- *The super-talented songwriter Cole Porter could be very **waspish** at times: one of his lyrics alludes to the large feet of a popular Swedish actress: "If you* *know Garbo, tell me the news/Is it a fact the Navy's launched all her old shoes?"*

8. Extant (EK-stant or ek-STANT)

This word offers a one-word way to say "still in existence."

- *Fossil records show us that many ancient forms of life were quite different from **extant** life.*

- *The fact that there are eighty **extant** manuscripts of Chaucer's poetry from the early fifteenth century testifies to his popularity.*

9. Insipid (in-SIP-id)

From the Latin for "not savory" or "not tasty," this adjective means just that—"tasteless" or "dull." You can use it to describe a certain food, or just about anything else that's bland, including someone's personality. The noun forms, **insipidity** and **insipidness**, are rarely used.

- *My chicken vindaloo was so **insipid** that I don't think I'll go back to Bombay Palace Cafe. I like my food to be spicier and more flavorful.*

- *Considering that he devoted himself to his job for over thirty years and was on such warm terms with his staff, Mr. Dobbs' good-bye speech at his retirement party was rather **insipid**.*

10. Quixotic (quik-ZOT-ik)

This adjective, meaning "overly idealistic," derives directly from the fictional Spanish hero Don Quixote, who overtly displays that trait. (The adjective takes on English pronunciation, while the Don retains the "kee-HOE-tay" pronunciation befitting the Man of La Mancha.)

- *Mr. Hanly admired his **quixotic** young student, so he spoke very gently when he said it might be difficult to win the Nobel Peace Prize as well as write a great novel before he was thirty-five.*

- *One side of Caitlin's personality is **quixotic,** but she tempers that with a highly practical streak.*

Quiz #1

CATEGORY A

Match each definition on the right with the appropriate word in the column on the left.

_____ epiphany   A. scold, take issue with

_____ capricious   B. make no longer necessary

_____ anthropoid   C. a sudden understanding,
                               a revelation

_____ obviate   D. flighty, given to acting on a whim

_____ remonstrate   E. resembling a human

CATEGORY B

Select a word from the list below that best fits each of the sentences on the next page. (One sentence calls for two words.) Some words won't be used at all.

quixotic	harbinger
extant	patrician
pique	vacillate
placate	clandestine

1. She wanted to buy a gift in an attempt to _____ the friend she feared she had offended.

2. She had a hard time deciding what to buy, tending to _____ between flowers and a CD.

3. He was in a fit of _____ because his _____ meeting place had been discovered.

4. He feared that the dark cloud was a _____ of bad weather.

5. The book was expensive, because there were only a few copies still _____.

CATEGORY C

1. The coach had expected his speech to galvanize the team; the players found his presentation insipid. What did the coach expect, and what happened?

2. The teacher said that Ann's interest in the subject proved to be ephemeral. What did the teacher mean?

3. Perhaps she's a bit capricious, but I wouldn't call her quixotic. Give examples of something she might do, and something she probably wouldn't.

4. The duke said that noblesse oblige did not require that he socialize daily with the proletariat. What did he mean?

5. The student's apology obviated the teacher's planned remonstration. Explain.

6
clean words

Whether it's your room or your conscience, getting things clean can take work. Some of these words have a generic sense, while others deal with more specialized forms of "cleaning."

1. Burnish (BURR-nish)

This verb refers to making shiny or glossy; it can be used literally or figuratively. (The second and third letters have switched places, but the first syllable is related to the first syllable of Brunhilda, the German warrior woman who was so shining in battle.)

- *Although Joey **burnished** the oil lamp until its metal shone, no genie appeared to grant him three wishes.*

- *Not content with three drafts of her memoir, Cassie **burnished** the prose until every page reminded the reader of poetry.*

2. Catharsis (ka-THAR-sis)

Greek tragedies, said the philosopher Aristotle, cause viewers to undergo a figurative cleansing—a catharsis—

of emotions such as pity and fear. We still use the word today to talk about Greek tragedy, and we also use it for any experience that leaves an individual with a feeling of release from emotional tension.

- *The innovative musical* The Gospel at Colonus *uses a gospel choir to express the viewers' sense of* **catharsis** *after the death of the protagonist, Oedipus.*

- *Stephen's argument with his dad at the Thanksgiving dinner table was embarrassing to the guests, but both father and son found it* **cathartic***; by the time the pumpkin pie was served they were cracking jokes together.*

3. Bowdlerize (BODE-ler-ize)

This verb has to do with literary cleansing. It comes from Thomas Bowdler (1754–1825), who published an expurgated version of Shakespeare "in which those words or expressions are omitted which cannot with propriety be read aloud in a family." It means to delete from a manuscript anything deemed offensive, or to skew the content in a certain way. The noun form is **bowdlerization**.

- *The novels of Henry Miller are too explicit to* **bowdlerize***; by the time a conservative editor finished removing offensive material, there would be little left.*

- *Horrified by the* **bowdlerization** *of the Shakespeare editions at her school, the English teacher collected them all and burned them.*

4. Meticulous (meh-TICK-u-lus)

This adjective emphasizes painstaking attention to detail. While it's always a compliment today, it has its roots in the Latin word for "fear."

- *The fact that Lei has a wild artistic imagination does not conflict with the **meticulous** nature of his drawing techniques.*

- *Willingness to give **meticulous** attention to details, and strong eyesight, are the chief requirements for those attempting the ancient art of making lace.*

5. Fastidious (fas-TID-e-us)

This adjective pushes **meticulous** (see #4) toward a further extreme. It can still be used in a positive context, but often moves over into meaning "overly exact" or "unnecessarily tidy."

- *Even as a small child, Fauntleroy was **fastidious**: his toys were arranged precisely on the shelf, and the teddy bear was in the exact middle of the bed.*

- *Some consider **fastidious** people unfortunate, for they are so seldom pleased with anything.*

*The novels of Henry Miller are too explicit to **bowdlerize**; by the time a conservative editor finished removing offensive material, there would be little left.*

6. Immaculate (im-MAK-you-let)

This adjective comes from the Latin word for "not blemished" and means "impeccably clean" or "flawless." Although the word is best known from the idea of "Immaculate Conception," the doctrine in the Roman Catholic Church that dictates that the Virgin Mary was conceived free from all stain of original sin, it is perfectly all right to use it to describe a more secular purity.

- *"I want this room to be **immaculate** before you leave," Mildred announced to her daughter Alex. "Pick up all the dirty laundry and put it in the hamper, make your bed, and vacuum the cookie crumbs off the carpet or you're not going anywhere!"*

- *Carrie's school record was **immaculate**. Her test scores were perfect; her grades were excellent; and she was involved in numerous extracurricular activities, including sports and community service work.*

7. Purge (perj)

This verb, which comes from the Latin word for "pure," means "to cleanse or purify." It can be used in many different contexts. One can be purged of sin (the word *purgatory*, for instance, describes a place of remorse or purging). It can be used in the law to mean "cleared of charges." It can mean "to get rid of impurities" in a more general way.

- *The vegetables at the health food store are carefully washed and **purged** of all of their impurities before being pressed into fresh juice at the juice bar.*

- *Orthodox Judaism requires that women be **purged** in a mikvah, a ritual purification bath, before the Sabbath prayers.*

8. Pristine (priss-TEEN)

This is another good adjective that means "clean and pure, free from dirt or decay." It also means "original or uncorrupted."

- *"This copy of Dante's* Inferno *is in **pristine** condition," said the rare-book dealer. "The binding is perfect and the pages are clean. It looks as if it has never been opened."*

- *After the masterful restoration work, the Renaissance frescoes seemed to return to their **pristine** condition.*

9. Quintessence (kwin-TESS-ence)

This noun refers to something that is not at any extreme except the extreme of being purely or perfectly itself. The origin of the word had the literal meaning of having been purified five (*quint*) times.

- *In his melancholy, Hamlet described mankind as being the "**quintessence** of dust."*

- *Andrea and Catherine are good examples of the **quintessential** student—one who is always curious, always looking to add knowledge onto what he or she already knows.*

10. Lustration (luss-TRAY-shun)

The most scholarly word of the ten, this noun refers to a ceremony of purification. Its better-known linguistic cousin is the word **luster**; thus, **lackluster** describes something or someone lacking in vitality.

- *The Greek chorus of the men of Thebes asked the oracle if the plague on the city could be lifted through prayer and **lustration**.*

- *"You get the work done, Smedley," said the overbearing boss, "but your **lackluster** attitude keeps you off the track to promotion."*

7 false words

There's truth at one end of the spectrum and falsehood at the other—in between, there's everything else. These words are helpful to describe those many and varying shades of gray.

1. Meretricious (mer-uh-TRISH-us)

A meretricious item attracts the viewer's attention but in a showy, vulgar manner. Appropriately enough, the adjective derives from the Latin word for "prostitute."

- *Fitzgerald's Jay Gatsby, who is described as being in the service of "a vast, vulgar, and **meretricious** beauty," is prone to excess: too much alcohol served at too many parties, too many unread books, even—some would say—too many shirts.*

- *"A little more restraint," said Kelly, "makes you more appealing. Any more sequins on that outfit and the effect will be positively **meretricious**."*

2. Pyrrhic (PEER-ik)

This adjective is most often used in the phrase *a pyrrhic victory,* meaning a technical win achieved at a high cost.

The word derives from an ancient Greek general named Pyrrhus, who defeated the Romans in 280 BC but lost nearly all his own troops in the process.

- *Daniel, in a rather rude manner, pointed out his teacher's mispronunciation of "tyranny" in front of the class; he was correct about her error, but I'd call it a **pyrrhic** victory since he needs her goodwill in writing his college recommendation.*

- *Some historians point out that, as most slave societies were able to abolish slavery without violence, the Union triumph in the American Civil War was somewhat **pyrrhic**.*

3. Innuendo (in-you-END-o)

This noun comes from the Latin for "hint" or "give a nod to." It means "a subtle or indirect expression." A synonym might be *insinuation*. It may refer to something true, but all too often it suggests a kind of half-truth associated with rumor or gossip. In a legal sense, it means "allegedly libelous or slanderous material."

- *"This article is full of **innuendo**," shouted the starlet. "I was not married in a secret ceremony in Las Vegas."*

- *The defense attorney in the murder trial attacked the prosecution's case as being based on **innuendo**, not fact.*

4. Disingenuous (diss-in-JEN-u-ous)

Don't play dumb with me! That's what someone who is disingenuous does. An **ingenue** is an innocent young woman, and a male or female pretending innocence is being disingenuous.

- "I had no idea I would hurt your feelings when I called you a total dunderhead," she said, smiling **disingenuously**.

- When former President Clinton defended himself from attack by saying much depended "on what the meaning of 'is' is," was he being a clever legal strategist or just being **disingenuous**?

5. Mendacity (men-DASS-ih-tee)

Mendacity is dishonesty, plain and simple. The adjective form is **mendacious**.

- Is the character of Dill in To Kill a Mockingbird **mendacious** because he is just basically dishonest, or because he wants to use his fabulous imagination?

- In Tennessee Williams' play Cat on a Hot Tin Roof, the characters Brick and Big Daddy have a memorable exchange about **mendacity**, each having good reason to be well-acquainted with the quality.

*Fitzgerald's Jay Gatsby, who is described as being in the service of "a vast, vulgar, and **meretricious** beauty," is prone to excess: too much alcohol served at too many parties, too many unread books, even—some would say—too many shirts.*

6. Chimera (ki-MEER-ah)

This noun denotes a scary female from Greek mythology. The mythological chimera was a fire-breathing monster: part lion, part goat, and part snake. A chimera became the more generalized word for any creature of the imagination, any unfounded concept. The adjective form, **chimerical,** may be seen more often today.

- *Sometime in the eighteenth century the concept of a giant sea snake ceased to be a **chimera** and became a zoological fact.*

- *Andrea traded in her **chimerical** hopes of becoming a second Madonna for work on an MBA degree.*

7. Travesty (TRA-vess-tee)

This noun originally meant "an exaggerated imitation of something, usually of a literary work." It has come to mean any grotesque parody of something, or a disastrous mockery. It comes from the French word for "disguise" or "parody."

- *"Allowing the murderer to go free is a **travesty** of justice," said the lawyer. "It is a gross misinterpretation of the law."*

- *The soccer game was a **travesty;** the Boston team, usually far superior to their opponents, was careless, clumsy, and thoughtless. It's no wonder they lost by two goals.*

8. Mirage (meer-AHZ)

Whether it's a literal vision of water imagined by the desperate crawler in the desert or a more figurative hope, this word is a good synonym for *illusion*, something imagined but insubstantial.

- *A variation on the cartoon of the water-seeker in the desert depicted a Martian eyeing a **mirage** at the horizon and crying, "Ammonia! At last, ammonia!"*

- *The **mirage** of financial security for life was brutally blasted for many people when their savings crumbled in the bank failure.*

9. Putative (PU-ta-tive)

This adjective describes something that is generally regarded as true, but has not been proven. *Supposed* would be a good synonym.

- *Because the **putative** father of the new baby refused to take a paternity test, the child grew up uncertain as to whether her father was a well-known politician.*

- *The novel* The Moonstone *has several **putative** authors, for the novel pretends to be a collection of documents, but the real author is Wilkie Collins.*

10. Sophistry (SOPH-is-tree)

If you engage in sophistry, you are arguing your case with superficially good reasoning that turns out to be full of holes. The **sophist** is out to display his or her cleverness and enjoys fooling others. The root word is the Greek word for "wisdom," but sophistry is a poor substitute for the real thing.

- *If Mr. Claxon wants to play the **sophist** with his friends, fine, but he has no business coming into a* *junior high classroom and misleading students not yet able to rebut his superficially clever logic.*

- *One may fool others with **sophistical** thinking, but one must be very clever not to indulge in self-deception.*

8
gloomy words

Do you want to talk about it? If you must be gloomy, you don't have to be silent. To deal verbally with a downcast state of mind, you have your choice of several words.

1. Lugubrious (lug-OO-brius)

This adjective means "gloomy," often to an exaggerated degree; it comes from the Latin word meaning "mournful."

- *Just because you had to miss the track meet is no reason to drag your **lugubrious** attitude around the hallways, making no attempt to get rid of your bad mood.*

- *The **lugubrious** tone of the card Lauren sent to Dan was more worthy of a sympathy note than the invitation to the movies that it was.*

2. Apathetic (ap-a-THET-ic)

Here's a useful adjective to describe someone who lacks feeling, lacks interest, has a bad case of "the blahs." It comes into English from the Greek root word "path" (feeling) and the prefix *a-* (absence of). The noun form is **apathy**.

- *Although Marie claimed to be **apathetic** about political disputes, she cared very much when the issue touched her life directly.*

- *The humor of the old joke line, "I'm not **apathetic**; I just don't care," requires that the hearer know the meaning of the key word.*

3. Saturnine (SAT-ur-nine)

This adjective means "gloomy," but with a bitterly sarcastic and mocking tone. The Roman god Saturn doesn't deserve such a melancholy or cynical term. Today many people happily bear his name on their cars, and in ancient times he presided over a very jolly festival called Saturnalia in late December. Saturn was not saturnine!

- *The judge's **saturnine** countenance increased the nervousness of the first-year lawyer.*

- *Many people think of* Gulliver's Travels *as a children's book, but careful readers will easily detect the **saturnine** temperament of its author, Jonathan Swift.*

4. Miasma (my-AZ-ma)

From the Greek word for "pollution" or "stain," this noun means "a poisonous atmosphere or influence." It originally referred to the atmosphere thought to arise from swamps or putrid matter.

- *The **miasma** of failure that hung in the locker room after the team lost the football game inspired* *the coach to launch into a pep talk about the lessons of failure.*

- *The title character of Henry James's Daisy Miller catches malaria after walking through the **miasmic** atmosphere in the Roman Forum at night.*

5. Funereal (fyu-NEER-e-ul)

As you'd guess, this adjective is related to the word *funeral*, but it now serves the purpose of describing a wider realm of gloom.

- *In the Victorian era, **funereal** customs were rigid and elaborate: there was even a special category of mourning jewelry considered acceptable to wear in the year following the death of someone close to you.*

- *As she entered the room to give her concession speech, Justine found her supporters slumped in **funereal** gloom. She tried to rally them with a cry of "Wait till next time! We've learned a lot in this campaign."*

Many people think of Gulliver's Travels *as a children's book, but careful readers will easily detect the **saturnine** temperament of its author, Jonathan Swift.*

6. **Dearth** (rhymes with *earth*)

The meaning of this noun is simple. There's not enough of something or maybe there's simply none of it. The origin is in the Middle English word for "costly," kept in the British use of *dear*—"I'd like to buy mince pies, but they're so dear lately."

- *The committee was surprised by the **dearth** of applicants for the Bedriomo Travel Grant. Isn't any student traveling this summer? Couldn't anyone use a little extra money?*

- *The problem with this party is that there's a **dearth** of mirth.*

7. **Melancholy** (mel-an-COLL-ee)

Today we're more likely to use the term *depression* for what an earlier era described with this word. It may have an easily defined cause, or it may be that state of mind expressed well in the opening line of Shakespeare's *Merchant of Venice*: "Indeed, I know not why I am so sad." The root words mean "black bile," and the condition can feel like a black hole.

- *Shakespeare's Hamlet is sometimes referred to as "the **melancholy** Dane" because of his deep soul-sickness.*

- *The comic valentine was addressed to "my **melancholy** baby" and made silly (and linguistically incorrect) puns having to do with melons and collies.*

8. Sepulchral (sep-ULL-krul)

It literally refers to a burial place—a grave or tomb, also known as a **sepulcher**. But it's often used to describe an exaggeratedly gloomy tone of voice, such as might be featured in a scary film featuring a phalanx of mummies.

- *The speaker in Poe's poem "Annabel Lee" refers to placing his beloved sweetheart in "the **sepulcher** there by the sea, / In her tomb by the sounding sea."*

- *Like many listeners, Alec reaches for the "off" button on the radio when a **sepulchral** voice starts intoning about products for incontinence.*

9. Morose (more-OSE)

This adjective describes someone who is gloomy, generally down in the dumps.

- *While there is little pleasure in the company of those who are **morose**, those who are unflaggingly cheery can also be tiring.*

- *Several of Shakespeare's characters are distinctly **morose**, beset by many worldly troubles.*

10. Crapulous (KRAP-u-lus)

This is a fancy adjective for that temporary type of gloom we've all read about—the hangover. Yes, it's a real word, with a respectable Greek origin.

- *The best scene in literature featuring a character in a **crapulous** condition is probably in Kingsley Amis's Lucky Jim.*

- *The census taker who knocked on the door of the **crapulous** Mr. Barkus did not have a pleasant few minutes ahead of him.*

9
government by…?

Put a group of people together and pretty soon some of them manage to gain power and control over the others. How do they structure their controlling group? People have done it in about every way you could imagine. We know about *democracy* (government by the people) and about a *republic* form of government (whereby representatives govern, as in our system). But humans have been very creative about inventing other ways to organize governments and power structures. Here are some useful words about what they've come up with.

1. Oligarchy (AH-luh-garky)

In a pure democracy, you have government by the people—all the people. But in an oligarchy, you have government by a few. Oligarchies may be hidden under another form of government or structure, as when a social class, a clique, or a group of cronies helps each other gain and retain power.

- *Soon after moving to the town, they found that a few powerful cronies—an **oligarchy**—wielded all the power.*

- *Many business and government organizations are **oligarchies** masquerading as democratic structures.*

2. Plutocracy (plu-TOCK-ruh-see)

A plutocracy is rule by the rich and powerful. It's another power structure that is often hidden beneath a more benign type of rule, as when the wealthiest people gain the controlling power in a democracy or republic. (Plutocracy and **plutocrat** are almost always used in a pejorative or negative sense.)

- *Some social scientists believe that the very rich have gained so much power that we are in danger of living in a virtual **plutocracy**.*

- *In the early twentieth century, **plutocrats** wielded immense power, and it appeared for a while that we might be on the road to becoming a **plutocracy**.*

3. Totalitarianism (toe-ta-la-TARE-ee-un-ism)

As its name suggests, this form of government exercises complete control over nearly all facets of its citizens' lives—their social and economic behavior surely, but often much more (e.g., education, religion, speech).

- *The fascist regimes of Italy and Germany were among the first **totalitarian** governments in our modern world.*

- *Books such as* Brave New World *and* 1984 *depict **totalitarian** societies.*

4. Meritocracy (mer-uh-TOCK-ruh-see)

In theory at least, power in a meritocracy is shared by the people who deserve it. An institution of higher learning is the most-common example of such a system.

- *Philosophers dream of living in a **meritocracy**, where people earn (or merit) influence based on ability and accomplishments.*

- *The college president believed that a **meritocracy** was the best power structure, but found it difficult to identify those who merited advancement.*

5. Stratocracy (struh-TOCK-ruh-see), also known as militocracy (mil-la-TOCK-ruh-see)

In this form of government, leaders of the armed forces are in control of the government (often following a military takeover, or coup).

- *It's for good reason that civilians are at the top of our military chains of command; this reduces the chance of a **stratocratic** government.*

- *Heads of government must beware of letting their top brass gain too much power, lest they find their societies converted to **militocracies**.*

As he grew older, Geronimo began to favor a gerontocracy.

6. Gerontocracy (jer-un-TOCK-ruh-see)

In a gerontocracy, the power is retained by the oldest people (in most cases, old men). The word probably comes from the Greek terms for "old man" and "rule."

- *As he grew older, Geronimo began to favor a **gerontocracy**.*

- *During the reign of the "Eight Immortals"—a **gerontocracy**—in Communist China, someone quipped that "the eighty-year-olds were calling meetings of the seventy-year-olds to decide which sixty-year-olds should retire."*

7. Nepotism (NEP-o-tizm)

This noun refers to favoritism shown to relatives in practices such as business matters. While it comes from the Latin word for "nephew," it now refers to any family member.

- *"My sister is better qualified for this job than anyone I know," lamented Edwina. "Too bad the company has a strict policy against **nepotism**."*

- *Colleges that give preference in admissions to children of alumni practice an open form of **nepotism**, which is outlawed in some companies.*

8. Anarchy (AN-ark-ee)

Confusion takes a political turn with this word. From the Greek for "without a ruler," anarchy is a noun that means "the absence of any form of political authority" or a more general "absence of order or control." The noun **anarchism** means something slightly different; it is a theory that all forms of government are oppressive and should be abolished. Someone who believes in anarchism is an **anarchist**.

- *When the principal called the teacher into the hallway, **anarchy** broke out in the classroom. The students began throwing spitballs and tossing papers out of the window.*

- *An avowed **anarchist,** Rachel was opposed to creating a student council in the middle school.*

9. Ochlocracy (ock-LOCK-ruh-see)

When all else fails, and no organized group can gain power, the result may be ochlocracy—rule by mobs.

- *When the government was overthrown and the new government could not gain control, things quickly devolved into **ochlocracy**.*

- *The refugees streamed across the borders, fleeing the violent mobs of the **ochlocracy**.*

10. Kakistocracy (kack-us-TOCK-ruh-see) and Kleptocracy (klep-TOCK-ruh-see)

We'll end this list with two interesting but unofficial words about government. Kakistocracy is government by the worst people, and kleptocracy describes a government in which control has been stolen—gained illegitimately through ballot-rigging or other means. And for a bonus, here's **interregnum** (in-tur-REG-num)—the period between reigns, as when one king dies and another is not immediately crowned.

- *If we fail to inform ourselves and vote, we may well end up living under a **kakistocracy**.*

- *Because of trouble with voting machines and vote-counting during the election, some people insist that the result was a **kleptocracy**.*

- *A few unscrupulous politicians tried to sneak changes into draft legislation during the **interregnum** between the conventions and the election, when they thought they'd be less likely to be caught.*

10 gallimaufry

This word (pronounced gal-uh-MAUF-ree) means "a stew, a mixture, a hodgepodge." It's thought to come from an Old French term meaning "to amuse yourself, to make merry." So here's a mixture for your merriment—and for expansion of your vocabulary.

1. Arcane (are-CANE)

We like mysteries, and may respect or envy people who understand things that are uncommon knowledge. This adjective means "known to or understood by only a very few people" (perhaps members of a select or secret group).

- *The tribal initiation involved revelation of **arcane** information about the jungle.*

- *She loved to learn about psycholinguistics and other **arcane** subjects.*

2. Vitriolic (vi-tre-AHL-ic)

Here's a particularly strong adjective that means "scathing" or "bitterly cruel." It's reserved for the most acidic humor or criticism. The noun form is **vitriol**.

- *The humor of comedian Lenny Bruce could be particularly* **vitriolic** *when he was mocking conventional mores and ideas.*

- *Put off by Charles's* **vitriol,** *Angela decided not to see him anymore, and began dating a very gentle pharmacist.*

3. Helical (HEL-la-k'l or HE-luh-k'l)

A **helix** is a spiral, so this word means "like or resembling a spiral." Screw threads are helical.

- *The DNA molecule has a double-**helix** shape—like a ladder that has been twisted.*

- *The Archimedes screw was a **helical** tube that, when inserted at an angle and turned, could lift water to a higher level.*

4. Eclectic (ek-LEK-tik)

From the Greek word for "select," this adjective means "made up from a variety of sources." The noun form is **eclecticism**.

- *Global Crossings, the new shop on the corner of Maple and Elm Streets, sells an **eclectic** mix of Far Eastern home furnishings, Latin American folk art, and Native American jewelry.*

- *A musician known for his **eclecticism,** Smiling Lemon Hawkins has included jazz, pop, and folk tunes on his new CD.*

5. Badinage (bad-in-AHZH)

We have a wide variety of ways we talk to each other, and this word can be just the right one when you want to identify the playful, back-and-forth banter of fun-loving friends.

- *He delighted in her company, and looked forward to their clever, teasing **badinage**.*

- *The high-school band played a number called "**Badinage** for Brass," in which the instruments tossed playful passages back and forth.*

*The new poetry anthology in Ms. Van Meer's ninth grade English class contains an **amalgamation** of poets from Europe, Asia, Latin America, and the Caribbean.*

6. Fecund (FEE-kund or FEK-und)

This word means "productive, capable of producing something" (such as offspring, fruit, ideas). It usually means "*highly* productive, producing heavily."

- *The **fecund** vines were heavy with dark, lush fruit.*

- *What a **fecund** mind she has—churning out clever ideas one after another.*

7. Amalgamate (ah-MAL-gam-ate)

This word, which may have come to us from Arabic, means "to mix or combine into a unified whole." The noun form is **amalgamation**.

- *The new poetry anthology in Ms. Van Meer's ninth grade English class contains an **amalgamation** of poets from Europe, Asia, Latin America, and the Caribbean.*

- *Tired of the disorganized array of papers on his desk, Mr. Candis asked his secretary to **amalgamate** them and put them in a file labeled "Desk Papers."*

8. Genome (GEE-nome)

This is the name for a full set of our genes—the material by which all our inheritable traits are passed along. The word was coined by a German botanist from *gen-* (gene) and *-ome* (from the ending of *chromosome*).

- *The mapping of the human **genome** was not possible until recent and startling scientific advances.*

- *The **genome** map offers great promise in preventing, curing, or ameliorating many inherited health problems.*

9. Germane (jer-MAIN)

We all know someone who veers off the topic at hand and starts talking about something unrelated—something that's not germane (relevant, related, appropriate) to the discussion.

- *We don't have a lot of time here, so please refrain from comments that are not **germane** to our topic.*

- *He didn't say much, but his remarks were invariably on-target, **germane,** and informative.*

10. Carapace (CARE-uh-pace)

In zoology, a carapace is a hard covering of some sort, like a turtle's shell. But it may be used figuratively to describe any protective covering.

- *Many crustaceans develop **carapaces** to protect them from predators.*

- *He was much criticized for ranting about unpopular beliefs, but he had gradually built a thick **carapace** to shield his psyche.*

Quiz #2

CATEGORY A

Match each definition on the right with the appropriate word in the column on the left.

_____ apathetic   A. a thick protective covering

_____ carapace   B. a heavy, oppressive atmosphere

_____ disingenuous C. perfectly clean, unspotted

_____ immaculate   D. describing a feeling of lack of enthusiasm

_____ miasma   E. not straightforward

CATEGORY B

Select a word from the list below that best fits each of the sentences on the next page. Some words won't be used at all.

anarchy	**arcane**
chimera	**dearth**
eclectic	**germane**
innuendo	**quintessence**

1. Is what you're reading about _____ to the paper you need to write?

2. Make your choice of sources _____. You don't want all information from one source.

3. I'm just trying to grasp the _____ of the subject, the facts that are really most important.

4. Just tell me the truth straight to my face. Don't keep engaging in _____ on the topic.

5. My hope for a high grade in chemistry the second quarter had seemed realistic, but it all turned out to be a _____ after I did so badly on the lab test.

CATEGORY C

1. Would you be likely to feel a sense of catharsis after a pyrrhic victory? Why or why not?

2. If you lived in a kakistocracy, would you be likely to feel saturnine much of the time? Why or why not?

3. That edition of Shakespeare is pristine, but I'm afraid it has been bowdlerized. Do you still want it? Explain.

4. Would you have more trouble dealing with a lugubrious friend than with a pal who was often vitriolic? Explain.

5. You and a friend engage in badinage about the advantages and disadvantages of living in a plutocracy. What's the conversation like?

11

helping words

"Mayday!"—the international radiotelephone distress call for help—is a delightful pun drawn from the French "m'aidez!" ("help me"). While the word *help* is itself directly descended from the Anglo-Saxon, many of the following helping words have their roots in Latin.

1. Redress (re-DRESS)

It doesn't refer to a literal change of clothing, but to a figurative "reclothing" of a situation—in short, an improvement, a remedy. It's used as both a noun and a verb, perhaps more frequently the latter.

- *Taxpayers are seeking **redress** for the drastic increases in property taxes that the county arbitrarily imposed last fall.*

- *In Shakespeare's play* Julius Caesar, *Brutus believes that the citizens of Rome want him to **redress** the loss of civic freedom brought about during Caesar's rule.*

2. Ameliorate (uh-MEEL-yur-ate)

This is a fancy verb that expresses the idea of improving. It comes from the Latin word for "better." The noun form is **amelioration**.

- *Joyce and George are seeking counseling in hopes of **ameliorating** their troubled relationship.*

- *Although the citizens of Ulubrae protested the unfair tax on fermented fish sauce to their consul, no **amelioration** ensued.*

3. Efficacy (EF-uh-kuh-see)

It's a slightly more interesting way of saying *effectiveness*; it describes something capable of bringing about a desired effect.

- *After two operations that brought no relief to his condition, Hugh began to lose faith in the **efficacy** of surgery.*

- *The **efficacy** of the tax on weasels and ferrets was proved negative when the county financial report showed only $42.00 was thus brought into the treasury.*

4. Emend (ee-MEND)

This verb means "to correct" or "to improve," particularly in reference to texts or documents. Don't confuse it with *amend*, which means "to add." The noun form is **emendation**.

- *The manuscript will go to press as soon as the copy editor has had a chance to **emend** the awkward introductions to each section.*

- *"I don't want a longer paper,"* explained Mr. Lombardo to the student. *"I want a better paper: we're talking about **emendations**, not amendments."*

5. Amnesty (AM-nus-tee)

An amnesty is a general pardon for those guilty of offenses or crimes. It comes from the same root word as *amnesia* in that it refers to official "forgetting" of the offense. It's sometimes used as well in an unofficial way.

- *The Elizabethtown Public Library offered a period of **amnesty** to all those who had overdue books: no fines would be charged for the entire month of February.*

- *Michael wrote his English teacher a note pleading for **amnesty** for his failure to read* A Tale of Two Cities *over the summer. "I'll teach you how to do a podcast," he winningly offered.*

In Shakespeare's play Julius Caesar, *Brutus believes that the citizens of Rome want him to **redress** the loss of civic freedom brought about during Caesar's rule.*

6. Elixir (ee-LIX-er)

An elixir is a liquid potion or medicine falsely believed to cure a multitude of ailments.

- *In earlier centuries, dishonest traveling salesmen peddled **elixirs** that would cure various ills—or so they promised, before they quickly left town.*

- *Could love be the true **elixir**? The composer Donizetti wrote an opera based on just such a premise.*

7. Mentor (MEN-ter or MEN-tor)

This synonym for a wise counselor or guide is an eponym taken from a character in Homer's *Odyssey*. (An eponym is a word whose origin is from the name of a person, whether real or—as in this case—fictional.) In the guise of Mentor, Athena is able to counsel and help Odysseus's son, Telemachus.

- *"While I never had Mr. Williams as a classroom teacher," said Lucia, "he was a wonderful **mentor** in all matters relating to acting."*

- *Although the company appointed an official **mentor** to each new summer intern, most of the young people found guidance in a more informal way.*

8. Protégé (male) or protégée (female) (PRO-teh-zhay)

This is the noun for someone whose career or progress is under the guidance ("protection") of an influential person, usually someone older and more experienced.

- *Although Elfrida was the more-qualified candidate, no one was surprised when Mr. Barone appointed his long-time **protégé**.*

- *Being a **protégé** of a powerful person has both plusses and minuses: where does loyalty end and dependency begin?*

9. Ancillary (AN-sill-air-ee)

From the Latin for "maidservant," this word was once used as a noun to mean "servant." It is now used as an adjective to mean "of secondary importance" or, alternatively, "something that is auxiliary or helpful to something else," such as a workbook is to a textbook.

- *"While you are in Paris," said Catherine's mother, "I'd like you to learn something about French art and architecture. Whether you actually learn to speak French is **ancillary**."*

- *On the first day of class, the teacher gave Catherine her art history textbook and several **ancillary** materials, including a collection of slides from the Louvre and a book about the French Impressionist painters.*

10. Retinue (RET-uh-nu)

This noun refers to a group of attendants, people who are there (they've been "retained") to tend to the needs of the more important person in their midst. You'll see it used in literature and history in reference to royalty, but in our officially more democratic era you can use it with an air of irony for someone who travels with a personal assistant, a bodyguard, and a manicurist.

For a synonym, modern slang might choose *posse*, but **entourage** (AHN-tour-ahjz)—those who "tour" with you—is a good, more formal choice.

- *The local stage version of* Hamlet *showed King Claudius with a follower or two, but the lavish film production filled the stage with his* **retinue.**

- *With so much human contact taking place online these days, it's not surprising that there's an email program named* **Entourage.**

12 jolly words

The flag of a pirate ship is called a "Jolly Roger"—surely an ironic use of this adjective. It's better associated with a smiley face than with a skull and crossbones.

1. Hedonist (HEE-dun-ist)

Derived from the Greek word for "pleasure," this noun denotes a person devoted to having a good time.

- *Eddie was something of a **hedonist**, living it up to all hours, until he surprised his friends by being accepted into a premed program and hitting the books with equal fervor.*

- *For Joe and Deedee, devout lovers of the printed word, a **hedonistic** day in London consists of visiting as many used bookstores as possible.*

2. Revelry (REV-uhl-ree)

A term for a loud good time, in the Dionysian sense. The verb, **revel** (REV-el), conveys a milder sense of the enjoying or relishing of anything, even a thought.

- *College officials are less than thrilled with the sounds of **revelry** streaming forth from on-campus residences every Saturday night.*

- *Liam **reveled** in the announcement that he had won the Lucio Piccolo poetry prize.*

3. Avuncular (uh-VUNK-u-ler)

As the second and third syllables suggest, this word describes a relationship with an uncle. By extension, it's used even more often to describe the kind, friendly manner of an unrelated man, a manner like the kind uncle you remember or wish you had had. (Aunts—time for a protest. There's no equivalent word for you. Take solace in the fact that in Latin even some uncles were left out, for the word referred only to an uncle on the mother's side!)

- *"I can't wait to see my brother and his son at the family barbecue," said Horace. "Nothing like renewing those fraternal and **avuncular** ties!"*

- *"McFadden's **avuncular** manner doesn't fool me," confided Sandra. "Underneath those corny jokes is a man conspiring to keep me from my next promotion."*

4. Ebullient (ee-BULL-yent)

This word describes an outward manner of high enthusiasm that would presumably come from a feeling of joy and high spirits. Its Latin root word is a verb meaning "to bubble up," so we might say you're figuratively "boiling over" with happiness when you're ebullient. The noun form is **ebullience**.

- *Lucretia's good mood was evident to us all from her **ebullient** greeting of each of us with a newly coined, affectionate nickname.*

- *When his accountant told him about the large tax refund he would receive this year, Mr. Gadda's resulting **ebullience** prompted him to make an immediate booking of a trip to Patagonia.*

5. Jocular (JOCK-u-lar)

A different variety of "smiley face" is represented by this word. *Jocular* has nothing to do with "jocks"; rather, it means "tending to make jokes." There are two close verbal cousins: **jocose** (joe-KOSE), which can be synonymous or can carry a more generalized meaning of "merry," and **jocund** (JOCK-und)—a somewhat more literary word meaning "lighthearted." All three have their roots in the Latin word for "joke."

- *Bartholomew was normally a serious fellow, but April Fool's Day brought out his **jocular** side.*

- *Lana's mood is somewhat more **jocose** than it was during exam week.*

- *If months had personalities, the month of May might be called **jocund**.*

*For Joe and Deedee, devout lovers of the printed word, a **hedonistic** day in London consists of visiting as many used bookstores as possible.*

6. Magnanimous (mag-NAN-im-us)

From the Latin word meaning "great soul," this adjective means "extremely generous and forgiving" and, more generally, "courageously noble in mind and heart." The noun form, a bit of a tongue twister, is **magnanimity**.

- *The **magnanimous** World Series losers congratulated and sent sandwiches to their opponents.*

- *"It was very **magnanimous** of you to lend us your home for the party," said the leader of the prom committee. "Not many people would be comfortable with three hundred teenagers in their living room."*

7. Euphoric (u-FORE-ik)

This word generally suggests an extreme of happiness, a "wow" feeling. (Its origins in Greek are more modest; it literally means "having good health," and indeed that should be a cause of great happiness.) The noun form is **euphoria**.

- *Mary Lou was understandably **euphoric** when she learned that she had just won the state lottery.*

- *Ms. Bosco claims that her cat feels **euphoric** when he gets a fair ration of catnip; while it's hard to know about an animal's feelings, jumping up and down and tossing the shreds of catnip in the air does indeed suggest intense happiness.*

8. Camaraderie (cam-uh-ROD-er-ee)

This happy noun refers to a sense of connection and fellowship among friends (think *comrade*). It derives from the French word for "roommate."

- *Even more than the pleasures of happy moments of shared recreation, Marilyn treasured most the sense of **camaraderie** that comes with working together with like-minded colleagues on a meaningful project.*

- *One of the paradoxes of war is that the greatest stress and danger can bring about the most intense **camaraderie** among the troops.*

9. Fete (rhymes with *bet*)

As a noun it's a celebratory party; as a verb it refers to the process of honoring someone with such a party. (Mentally supply an s and you see the root of *feast* or *festival*.)

- *The lovely old church in the English countryside had held its June **fete** for an unbroken run of sixty-three years without being rained out.*

- *On her sixtieth birthday Violetta's friends **feted** her with sprays of orchids, a case of champagne, and a cake bearing the message "The best is yet to be."*

10. Joie de vivre (zhwa duh VIVR)

This phrase is an immigrant from France, an *émigré*, we should say. Its meaning is simple—a sense of deep joy at the simple fact of being alive.

- *Although Hugh claims he's happy, his stiff body language and unsmiling face rob him of the impression of any sense of **joie de vivre**.*

- *The song "Life Is a Cabaret" vividly expresses the character's innate sense of **joie de vivre**.*

13

-id words

You surely know and use lots of words ending in -id, including the Freudian term id itself. Here are a few more that are useful, with a mixed bag of meanings—about the only thing they have in common is their last letters.

1. **Squalid** (SKWA-lid)

This adjective means "dirty or wretched," caused by poverty or negligence. It can also mean dirty in the sense of being morally repulsive. The noun form is **squalor**.

- *When he first joined the Peace Corps, Paul was horrified by the **squalor** in which the natives lived. Many of them slept on the floor in mud huts and had no electricity or flush toilets.*

- *The principal decided to ban several of the books on the reading list because he considered the material too **squalid** for high school freshmen.*

2. **Fetid** (FET-id)

If you want to describe something that smells bad, you could say it's malodorous, or maybe unaromatic.

But if it smells really bad, you may want to stretch all the way to *fetid*—usually reserved for rotting or putrid stuff.

- *The lost explorer spent days slogging through the **fetid** swamp.*

- *As the monster closed in upon her, the maiden was enveloped in its **fetid** breath.*

3. Sordid (SOR-did)

Something that's sordid is not just physically dirty, it's likely to be morally or ethically foul as well. In a slightly different meaning, it's sometimes applied to wretched conditions or surroundings, as in a slum.

- *We had thought of him as a pillar of the church and community, until the **sordid** details of his secret life came out.*

- *As she walked among the **sordid** shacks and shelters of the refugees, tears came to her eyes.*

4. Torpid (TOR-pid)

Torpid means "sluggish"—slower than slow, moving very little if at all. It can apply to mental as well as physical slowness.

- *Technically speaking, bears don't hibernate; they just become very **torpid**.*

- *As it cooled, the lava became increasingly **torpid**.*

5. Sapid (SAP-id)

Sapid can mean "having perceptible taste, not tasteless."

But it usually suggests something stronger—"having a distinctly pleasant taste"—or, when applied to nonfood things, "giving other kinds of pleasant sensations."

- *Suzanne certainly served a **sapid** soup.*

- *The **sapid** conversation after dinner was a bonus.*

> *As the monster closed in upon her, the maiden was enveloped in its **fetid** breath.*

6. Acrid (ACK-rid)

This word means "having a sharp, bitter taste or smell," and often suggests irritation (as of the eyes or nose).

- *As Pierre ran from the field, the **acrid** smell of gunpowder penetrated his nostrils.*

- *The **acrid** taste of the berries told him that they were inedible, and perhaps poisonous.*

7. Rancid (RAN-sid)

Rancid comes from the same Latin root as *rancor*, but is used slightly differently. It means "repugnant" or "nasty," but it doesn't describe people, only their remarks or behavior. It can also be used to describe food that has gone bad.

- *After two weeks in a warm refrigerator, the milk was **rancid**.*

- *The valedictorian's **rancid** remarks about the school's curriculum embarrassed the principal at the graduation ceremony.*

8. Vapid (VAP-id)

No acridity here. Anything that's vapid is dull, tasteless, lifeless, boring. (The word is related to *vapor*—and there's not much substance to that, either.)

- *The **vapid** conversation put her into a near-torpid state.*

- *Some people seem to like the parlor games, but she found them completely **vapid**.*

9. Flaccid (FLAS-id or FLAK-sid)

It's from the Latin for "flabby" and that's what it means. It can be used in the literal or the figurative sense.

- *The polio he suffered as a child left his leg muscles **flaccid**, but Wilfrid has not let wearing leg braces stop him from an active life and a successful career.*

- *Driving cross-country together, Grace and Emily kept up a nonstop, animated conversation about childhood, books, men, cats, careers, and life in general; the exchange became **flaccid** only when physical fatigue set in.*

10. Gravid (GRAV-id)

Gravid means "pregnant, carrying eggs or a fetus."

- *When the woman turned to go, her profile clearly showed that she was **gravid**.*

- *The fisherman held up the **gravid** salmon to show its distended, yellowish belly.*

14

lovers' words

All right, we admit it. The title of this chapter is designed purely to get your attention. But the literal truth is that all ten of these words are taken from Shakespeare's *Romeo and Juliet*. We haven't chosen the fancy sixteenth-century words such as *cockatrice* that are intriguing but not very useful today. (A cockatrice is a magical creature both roosterlike and lizardlike whose look could turn you to stone.) These words could appear in any twenty-first-century newspaper.

1. Pernicious (per-NISH-us)

Something deadly, dangerous, or destructive might be termed *pernicious*. You may have heard it in the name of the disease *pernicious anemia,* a particularly threatening form of anemia. *Deleterious* might be a good synonym.

- *"This form of the bacteria is particularly **pernicious**,"* explained Dr. Epstein. *"Just when we think we've developed a medicine to counteract it, it mutates into a newer, more deadly form."*

- *Supersize Me is a documentary vividly showing the **pernicious** effects of a diet made up primarily of meals from fast-food joints.*

2. Posterity (pos-TER-uh-tee)

Posterity refers to the generations that will come after you—whether your own possible descendants or the more impersonal people who belong to later eras. The *post-* part of the word suggests "after."

- *Those who encourage us to be aware of our treatment of the environment definitely have **posterity** in mind: we must, they say, be good stewards of this planet.*

- *The Bible story about Abraham states that all mankind shall be blessed through his **posterity**.*

3. Inauspicious (in-aw-SPISH-us)

This adjective is the negative of *auspicious,* which refers to a favorable sign or omen. Romeo and Juliet were, alas, more visited by those unfavorable signs.

- *The old tradition of a new husband carrying his bride across the threshold was designed to prevent the possibility of the bride **inauspiciously** stumbling as she entered her new home.*

- *How **inauspicious** would it be if a man carrying the woman in his arms should stumble under the burden of the extra weight?*

4. Heretic (HERR-uh-tik)

Originally, this noun referred to a person who dissented from the official beliefs of the established religion of a certain time and place. Today you'll also see it used to refer more generally to disagreement with majority opinion.

- *In order to avoid prosecution as a **heretic**, Galileo was forced to make an official disavowal of his discovery of scientific truth.*

- *"Sorry to make so **heretical** a statement," said Andrew lightly, "but I don't want hot dogs at our Fourth of July picnic. Might we have beef Wellington?!"*

5. Unwieldy (un-WEEL-dee)

This adjective describes something that's awkward to manipulate with grace. The positive adjective seems to have dropped from the language, but you'll occasionally hear the verb form **wield**—"to handle something well," literally or figuratively.

- *The **unwieldy** nature of the computer software made the program unappealing to all but the most technically adept.*

- *Ms. Pappas may not have an imposing title in her company, but she **wields** a lot of power behind the scenes.*

*The old tradition of a new husband carrying his bride across the threshold was designed to prevent the possibility of the bride **inauspiciously** stumbling as she entered her new home.*

6. Garish (rhymes with *parish*)

An adjective that describes something loud (in color or design), flashy, or glaring.

- *The shocking pink shirt worn with the chartreuse pants certainly caught the eye; only the addition of an orange belt could have made Mason's outfit more garish.*

- *The community of Oldest Oaks was horrified when the new residents painted their picket fence fire-engine red. The Neighborhood Association is sending Mrs. Oldschool around to discuss with them their garish taste.*

7. Prodigious (pro-DIJ-us)

If it's prodigious, it's huge, enormous.

- *Emily Dickinson lived a very quiet life in Amherst, Massachusetts, but her talent for writing poetry was prodigious, as was her life's work—more than 1,700 poems.*

- *Did Richie really eat two pints of chocolate ice cream? How could such a small child have so prodigious an appetite?*

8. Nuptials (NUPP-chuls)

If it ends in an s, it's a noun referring to a wedding, a marriage ceremony. Without the s, it's an adjective.

- *Romeo and Juliet's nuptials were celebrated in a secret ceremony—no wedding cake! no flowers!—performed by the sympathetic Friar Lawrence.*

- *Some skeptics believe that **nuptial** events have gotten out of hand today: does the confirmation of a couple's love for each other require that thousands of dollars be spent?*

9. Portentous (por-TENT-us)

This word suggests someone or something carrying a sign, a portent, of the threats of the future. A second meaning laps over into the pretentiously weighty, the pompous.

- *Sandy's midterm grades were passing but hardly **portentous** of a great year: she had three Cs and two Ds.*

- *When Mr. Jaggers speaks, his words bear a **portentous** air, as if what he has to say is highly meaningful to us all.*

10. Descry (dih-SCRY)

This verb comes to us from the French word for "to call out." It means "to catch sight of something that is difficult to see" or "to discover something by very careful scrutiny." It should not be confused with *decry,* which comes from the same French root but means "to openly condemn."

- *In the dusky distance, Marlowe **descried** a ship heading out toward the horizon, its sails golden in the sunset.*

- *After carefully examining the hieroglyphics in the cave, Indiana Jones **descried** directions that would lead directly to the secret vault containing the treasures of the lost ark.*

15 hodgepodge

Like the *farrago* and *gallimaufry* sections, this chapter offers you ten words united only by the fact that they are all interesting, and all useful.

1. **Feral** (FER-ul)

This adjective can describe either an animal in the wild or one returned to living in such a state. It can also describe human behavior that is more like the savagery of an animal.

- *Brad and Susanna, ardent cat lovers, wanted to adopt one of the **feral** cats prowling the garbage dump, but they worried about the response of Moggy and Lily, their pampered Persians.*

- *The **feral** smile of the salesperson was almost more disturbing than a leer, thought Candace.*

2. **Hirsute** (HEER-sute)

This unusual word means "hairy," often unusually so. It derives directly from Latin.

- *The **hirsute** face made it difficult to tell if the creature in the horror film was meant to be human or only partly human.*

- *The giggling girls at the swimming pool admitted that they were trying to decide which of the boys had the most **hirsute** back.*

3. Lurid (LOOR-id)

This adjective meaning "causing shock or horror, gruesome" gains its overkill effect through a glaring, unsavory sensationalism. Perhaps anticipating the potential effect of something lurid, its origin is the Latin word for "pale."

- *"Please, spare me the **lurid** details of the horrible things Rosemary said to you. They're just too painful to hear," Luke said sympathetically to Nora.*

- *The **lurid** headlines of the tabloid papers blazoned forth phrases like "body parts" and "sex fiend."*

4. Aesthetic (es-THET-ik)

This adjective refers to the perception or appreciation of beauty. One who values aesthetics is an **aesthete**.

- *Those who want to be architects must have a very practical sense of how buildings function, but they must also have a strong sense of **aesthetics**; no one wants an ugly building, no matter how practical it might be.*

- *Bea is a complete **aesthete**: her kitchen toaster barely makes a piece of bread light tan, but she defends the appliance on the grounds that "the* *pink stripe across the middle makes it look really pretty."*

5. Contumely (KON-toom-lee)

Though it looks like an adverb, this word is a noun that means "rudeness" or "arrogance." You won't see it often these days, unless you're reading a nineteenth-century novel, or if you're in a courtroom, where it is used to describe behavior that constitutes being in contempt of court. The adjective form is **contumacious**.

- *"If you continue with this **contumely**," Woolsey asserted, "I shall have to take you home from the ball. Such discourteous remarks are inappropriate, especially from a respectable girl."*

- *The defendant's outburst of hostility towards the judge was considered **contumacious** behavior, and he was severely punished for it.*

*"If you continue with this **contumely**," Woolsey asserted, "I shall have to take you home from the ball. Such discourteous remarks are inappropriate, especially from a respectable girl."*

6. Cryptic (KRIP-tik)

A crypt is a place where bodies or treasure may be hidden away. As an adjective, *cryptic* describes that which has a hidden or a puzzling meaning.

- *The pirates puzzled over the **cryptic** markings on the map, longing to believe a store of gold doubloons was waiting for them on the island.*

- *Rory's airs of superiority and **cryptic** utterances such as "Some day you'll understand" do little to win friends.*

7. Incarnation (in-car-NAY-shun)

Religiously speaking, this noun means "a fleshly version of the divine." Thus, in Christianity, it refers to Mary's conception of Jesus—and the initial letter is capitalized. More generally, it's used for the giving of bodily form to something abstract. The adjective form, **incarnate**, describes something that has been given form.

- *F. Scott Fitzgerald intensifies the religious feel of Gatsby's near-worship of Daisy when he writes, "He kissed her and the **incarnation** was complete."*

- *"You don't have to look at me as if I were the devil **incarnate** when I suggest going off your diet long enough to have a bite of my birthday cake," said Angela huffily to her friend Adele.*

8. Ecclesiastical (ek-LEEZ-ee-ASS-tik-al)

This adjective means "of or relating to a church" or "appropriate for use in a church." The noun form, **ecclesiastic**, means "a minister" or "priest."

- *Dressed in **ecclesiastical** robes and carrying a book of hymns, the bishop stood out in the crowd of children and parents at the school's December Christmas party.*

- *Because **ecclesiastics** from all over the world were in Rome to attend a special mass at the Vatican, it was impossible to obtain a hotel room at a reasonable price anywhere in the city.*

9. Esoteric (ess-oh-TER-ik)

This word refers to something that's known to only a few—perhaps members of a select group, or those few able to comprehend it.

- *The word "**esoteric**" is not a common word, but it is far less **esoteric** than the word "omphaloskeptic"— "meditating while staring at your navel." Now that's **esoteric**.*

- *Joelle, not being a sports fan, is intrigued by real sports enthusiasts who exchange **esoteric** bits of lore such as "most home runs hit by a left-handed batter being pitched to by a left-handed pitcher."*

10. Prehensile (pre-HEN-sul)

This interesting adjective describes something that's well-adapted to grasping, to holding on to. It may be the tail of a kinkajou or the brain of a brilliant person. The Latin root is the same as you find in words like *apprehend* and *comprehend*.

- *Eli wondered why his little brother's toes were so **prehensile**: he could pick up a pencil with them, a feat he flaunted in front of his flat-toed sibling.*

- *Samuel Johnson's mind was wonderfully **prehensile**: when he read a book he could quickly incorporate its substance into his store of knowledge.*

Quiz #3

CATEGORY A

Match each definition on the right with the appropriate word in the column on the left.

_____ ameliorate   A. gaudy, overdone, crudely showy

_____ esoteric   B. to make better, improve

_____ ancillary   C. known to only a select few

_____ garish   D. adapted for grasping, like a monkey's tail

_____ prehensile   E. accompanying, additional, not a central element

CATEGORY B

Select a word from the list below that best fits each of the sentences on the next page. (One sentence calls for two words.) Some words won't be used at all.

mentor	euphoric
feral	nuptials
ebullient	cryptic
protégé	elixir

1. People may think that polar bears are cuddly, but they're really _____ animals.

2. We all loved Bucky for her high-spirited, _____ dancing and singing.

3. The young artist was proud to be chosen as a _____ of the elderly sculptor, who was to be his _____ for several years.

4. The _____ feeling from the drugs did not wear off until hours after the surgery.

5. He read the _____ note, but didn't understand it.

CATEGORY C

1. The judge said that in order to redress an earlier judgment, amnesty for the prisoners was in order. What did he mean, and how should the prisoners feel about what he said?

2. The veterinarian noticed the gravid condition of three of Mr. Ailurophile's four cats. Describe the appearance of the Ailurophile home in the near future.

3. She was known for her joie de vivre; she was not considered a hedonist. How did she probably live?

4. The couple's spat was inauspicious, in view of the planned nuptials. Explain.

5. The avuncular teacher helped develop a feeling of camaraderie among his students. What was he like, and how did the students feel about the class?

16 lying words

It's been said that the Inuit have lots of words for snow, because they live among so much of it. What does that say about the fact that we have many words about lies and lying? In examining some of these—and a few about *not* lying—we'll start with a mild, positive one, and end with a couple of more serious negative terms.

1. Veracity (vuh-RASS-uh-tee)

If you're someone with a reputation for veracity, you're someone who tells the truth, whose word can be depended on. Unfortunately, this quality is often noted by its absence—in other people, of course, not you or me. Its opposite is *mendacity* (see Chapter 7).

- *Madam, are you questioning the **veracity** of my expense-account report?*

- *She's an unusual person—a political leader who is known for her **veracity**.*

2. Temporize (TEMP-er-ize)

From the Latin for "to pass one's time," this verb now has a slightly more sinister quality. It means "to act evasively in order to gain time or to avoid an argument."

- *The congressman **temporized** during a discussion of stem-cell research at a White House conference in order to delay the vote and create more time for his committee members to lobby opponents of the upcoming bill.*

- *In an effort to help their accomplice steal some chips from the corner deli, the two hoodlums **temporized** with the man at the cash register, distracting him with stories about the old neighborhood.*

3. Dissemble (dis-SEM-bull)

A dissembler doesn't usually tell outright lies, but conceals his true nature behind false words or deliberately misleading behavior.

- *The congregants were deeply disappointed to learn that the deacon had been **dissembling**, and had taken the offering and eloped with the preacher's daughter.*

- *He wanted to go into politics, so he took courses in drama to perfect his already significant **dissembling** skills.*

4. Subterfuge (SUB-ter-fuje)

The Latin root of this noun means "to escape secretly," but the word, like *ruse*, has come to mean "any secret plan or strategy."

- *"Telling me you had to work late last night was pure **subterfuge**," Alyssa shouted at her husband. "I know you were out playing cards with the boys to avoid having dinner with my mother."*

- *Through careful **subterfuge**, including dipping his thermometer into a cup of hot tea when his mother wasn't looking, Harvey managed to convince his parents that he was far too sick to go to school.*

5. Circumlocution (sir-cum-lo-CUE-shun)

This word literally means "talking around the point," and is sometimes used to describe speech by someone who isn't lying, just *logorrheic* (given to talking way too much). But it's very often used to mean "an intentional use of many words as a way of getting around the truth."

- *The reporter asked if all the talk about discussing, considering, and appointing a committee was just **circumlocution** for the fact that no real action was planned.*

- *Silent Cal Coolidge was known for his short, direct answers; he was not given to **circumlocution**.*

*Hannibal the cannibal was making a **double entendre** when he said he was having an old friend for dinner.*

6. **Equivocation** (ee-KWIV-uh-KAY-shun)

An equivocation is another form of not-quite-lie that nevertheless can be used to deliberately mislead. As the *equi-* suggests, it says a little of this, a little of that, so the listener can't be sure of the intent.

- *The skillful candidate's artful **equivocations** led people on both sides of the issue to conclude that he agreed with them.*

- *Some salesmen and office-seekers seem to make a vocation out of **equivocation**.*

7. **Double entendre** (DUB-ble ahn-tahn-druh)

Not all misleading words are bad, and here's a case in point. The double entendre is a word or phrase used in such a way that it can have a double meaning—one of them usually having sexual connotations. Such wordplay can be fun—a source of pleasure, a subtle display of clever wit. As a friend used to say, a dirty mind is a joy forever.

- *The teacher was never sure if Randy was making **double entendres**, but his sniggering classmates knew.*

- *Hannibal the cannibal was making a **double entendre** when he said he was having an old friend over for dinner.*

8. **Canard** (kuh-NARD)

Canard is an interesting word—it has three definitions. It can name a kind of duck, a projection on an aircraft wing, or a falsehood. In the third sense, a canard is usually intended to malign another person, to damage a reputation. It's not in common use, except in a humorous sense.

- *The offended gentleman insisted that the comment was a base **canard**, and demanded an apology.*

- *The speech was short on policy statements, long on **canards** lobbed at the opposing party.*

9. Tergiversate (ter-JIV-er-sate)

Literally, "to turn one's back on—to leave—a cause formerly supported." It can also be used to refer to speaking evasively, hoping to disguise one's meaning. One linguist puts it well in saying the word applies whether one is "ducking or weaving."

- *In Dickens's A Tale of Two Cities the unreliable character John Barsad fears he will be apprehended in France despite "his utmost **tergiversation**."*

- *President George H. W. Bush is remembered for his clever phrase, "Read my lips. No new taxes," but not everyone remembers that he later **tergiversated** on that issue.*

10. Subreption (sub-REP-shun)

We'll end the list with a word that's not often heard, but that has a niche where it can be just the right term. When you want to say that a person isn't exactly telling a direct lie, but is clearly and deliberately misleading, then *subreption* is the word you want. The adjective form is **subreptious**.

- *He's being **subreptious**—intentionally misrepresenting the truth through calculated omission of information.*

- *Too late they discovered that the fund managers were engaging in **subreption**—cooking the books to give the clients and auditors a picture that was much rosier than the truth.*

17 money words

There's an old saying—"money talks"—but it's equally true that we talk a lot about money. Here are some words to use in such conversations.

1. **Parsimonious** (par-sih-MOAN-ee-us)

This adjective comes from the Latin word that means "to spare," and it is the opposite of *magnanimous* (see Chapter 12). Someone who is parsimonious is excessively stingy. The noun form is **parsimony** (PAR-sih-moan-ee).

- *In order to save money, the **parsimonious** director of the orphanage refused to serve meat to the children more than once a week.*

- *Knowing her boss's **parsimony**, Nina did not ask for a raise, despite weeks of overtime work during the holidays.*

2. **Penurious** (pen-YUR-ee-us)

From the Latin meaning "want," this adjective means both "stingy, unwilling to spend money" and "poverty-stricken or destitute" (another good word for "poor"). The noun form is **penury**.

- *During the Great Depression, millions of Americans were reduced to a **penurious** lifestyle.*

- *Suffering disease, hunger, and **penury**, the homeless man sought help in a shelter; he didn't have enough money to buy himself a meal.*

3. Mendicant (MEND-ih-kant)

Mendicant, which may be used as a noun or adjective, is a formal term for a beggar. It derives from the Latin word for "needy" and an associated root for "physical defect."

- *Jon has been reading about **mendicant** friars, those who took an oath of poverty and depended on their belief in the providence of God and the kindness of others for their very survival.*

- *Laurie and Lily had seen beggars in large cities in the United States, but they were unprepared for the number of **mendicant** children coming up to them on their foreign travels last summer.*

4. Pecuniary (puh-KYOON-ee-air-ee)

From the Latin word for "property" or "wealth," this adjective simply means "having to do with money." One could say that all of the words on this list are "pecuniary words." A word with a similar meaning is *fiscal* (see #10).

- *After his wife died, Mr. Stevenson hired an accountant to deal with all of his **pecuniary** matters. He* had left all of the household finances to her and had no idea how to pay all of the bills.

- *The chief financial officer of the company was in charge of all **pecuniary** matters, including salaries, bonuses, stock options, and budgetary issues.*

5. Solvent (SOL-vent)

This adjective means "able to meet financial obligations." Someone who is solvent may not be rich, but is able to pay the bills. On the other hand, people who are **insolvent** are not able to cover their debts. The noun form is **(in)solvency**, but you can also refer to a bankrupt person as an **insolvent**.

- *Because they had no insurance, the Smith-Walcotts were **insolvent** when their house burned down in an accidental fire; they were forced to move in with relatives.*

- *"We're finally **solvent**!" exclaimed Horace to his new wife. "My new job will enable us to get a mortgage on a home and pay off our student debts."*

*In Macbeth a starless night is poetically described this way: "There's **husbandry** in heaven. Their candles are all out."*

6. Affluent (AF-floo-ent)

An adjective that means "rich, prosperous, wealthy," it comes from the Middle English word for "flowing." The money flows freely for affluent people. The noun form is **affluence**.

- *Gold River Estates is an **affluent** neighborhood. Every house has a swimming pool, a three-car garage, and a five-acre plot of land surrounding it.*

- *The psychologists are doing research on the impact of **affluence** on teen behavior. Their studies indicate that adolescents who come from upper-middle-class families face different issues than teenagers from lower-income neighborhoods.*

7. Remuneration (re-MYUN-er-AY-shun)

This is a noun that means "payment for goods or services provided." Salary is remuneration for work done, for example. The verb form is **remunerate**. A good synonym is *recompense*.

- *The hospital offered Caroline ample **remuneration** for her work in the intensive-care unit, because the hours were long and the schedule was very demanding.*

- *Carmen considered $20 per hour to be a fair **remuneration** for babysitting the Harrisons' four-year-old son, Irving, because he was very demanding and never went to bed when he was told.*

8. Lucrative (LOO-kra-tive)

This adjective means "yielding money or profit." Another word for money is **lucre**; however, it generally has a negative connotation associated with money that comes from greed, as in the mention of "filthy lucre" in the Bible (Titus 1:11). In fact, the word comes from the Latin root for "avarice."

- *"Plastics is a very **lucrative** business, Benjamin," said Mr. Robinson. "You should consider a career in a field that will make you rich."*

- *The miser surveyed his **lucre** and rubbed his hands greedily. "I'm rich! Rich!" he exclaimed.*

9. Husbandry (HUS-bun-dree)

This is an old-fashioned word, one you're unlikely to see very often these days. In its older sense it's a synonym for *thrift*, the ability to manage money and resources well. It sounds like the familiar word for the complement to a wife, since the Old Norse root referred to a man who owned land or managed a farm, but it came to be used for any man. The first sentence shows its verb form, **husband**, which retains the "thrifty" sense.

- *The marathon runner knew he had to **husband** his strength: if he gave his all at the halfway point, he'd never finish the race.*

- *In Macbeth a starless night is poetically described this way: "There's **husbandry** in heaven. Their candles are all out."*

10. Fiscal (FISS-kul)

This adjective can refer to finances in general and to government finances in particular. Its origin comes from the homely Latin word for "money basket."

- *The presidential candidate promised to improve the country's **fiscal** practices and thus bring about a stronger economy.*

- *While the school operates on the customary academic calendar, its **fiscal** year runs from July 1 to June 30 of the following year.*

- *Being asked to work in a cubicle beside the woman who had, in private life, betrayed him was somewhat **traumatic** for Percival.*

5. Schadenfreude (SHAD-en-froid-deh)

This noun comes from the German words for "damage" and "joy" and means "a pleasure derived from the misfortune of others."

- *Reveling in a bit of **schadenfreude**, Oliver was happy to see his parents blame his brother for the Ming vase the boys broke while playing catch in the living room. He was tired of being the one who always got in trouble.*

- *Although she didn't want to admit to her **schadenfreude**, Abby was happy to hear that everyone but her failed the math final; she thought it would make her seem especially smart to her teacher.*

> "It **harrows** me with fear and wonder," says Hamlet when, on the dark battlement of the castle, he first sees the ghost of his father.

6. Ostracize (OS-truh-size)

If you ostracize people, you make them pariahs (see below). This verb has the meaning of "expelling a person from a community," either literally or figuratively. Like many words and practices, this one came from ancient Greece, where a citizen could be forced to leave a city by vote of his peers. Not yet having paper, the citizens voted with shards of pottery—*ostraka,* forerunners of the modern "blackball." The noun form is **ostracism**.

- *Although the charges of sexual harassment against Mr. Larrabee have been dropped, he continues to be **ostracized** by a number of people in his workplace.*

- *To help her psychology students understand the power of social **ostracism,** Ms. Ewalt had her class participate in an experiment: on a regularly scheduled basis, each member of the class spent two days being shunned by others—no communication, no sharing of a lunchroom table.*

7. Pariah (puh-RYE-uh)

This noun refers to a social outcast, someone not accepted in his or her society. The word comes into English from Tamil, a language of southern India, where it refers more specifically to an "Untouchable," a member of the lowest caste.

- *Mark Twain calls Huckleberry Finn the "juvenile **pariah** of the village."*

- *After Aaron told the teacher about Ann's misdoings, he was treated like a **pariah** by classmates who felt "ratting someone out" was the worst possible offense.*

8. Tribulation (trib-u-LAY-shun)

This noun refers to a hardship, an affliction, a form of suffering. It's not related to *tribes* or *tribunes* or *tributes*. Its surprising (to most of us, at least) origin is the Latin word for "threshing sledge"—a device that pressed on the wheat just as an affliction might press or oppress your spirit. It's sometimes used in a specialized sense within the Christian religion as a period of great suffering for believers.

- *Those working for a greater degree of racial equality in the 1960s were sustained in their **tribulations** by their belief that this important change would come.*

- *When Martin went to the administration of his school to protest the absence of a soft drink machine, the principal said gently, "Martin, I don't think that going without a cola for six hours ranks as one of the great **tribulations** of all time."*

9. Sadism (SAY-dism)

This word suggests pleasure in inflicting pain on others. It's in that category of words called eponyms—words whose origin is from the name of a real person. In this case it's the infamous French writer the Marquis de Sade. The adjective form is **sadistic**.

- *Do those photographs of military guards taking delight in humiliating their prisoners move us from the brutal realities of war to the unacceptable horror of **sadism**?*

- *Dr. McLeod is a wonderful teacher, but some of her students enjoy accusing her of being **sadistic** because* *of the rigor of her assignments and the challenge of her expectations.*

10. Masochism (MASS-uh-KIZm)

Is it possible to take pleasure in being abused and humiliated? Complicated psychiatric case studies answer in the affirmative, but the word is often used now in a milder, exaggerated sense. Like *sadism,* this noun is an eponym, deriving from the name of a nineteenth-century Austrian novelist. The noun form, **masochist,** is used to refer to a person who displays masochism. The adjective form is **masochistic.**

- *You're taking differential calculus from that tough teacher? You must be a **masochist.***

- *People who play golf—with its frequent frustrations—must have **masochistic** tendencies.*

19

personality types

"It takes all kinds of people to make a world," the altruist said. "Yes," replied the cynic, "and they're damned sure all here."

1. Altruist (AL-tru-ist)

The root of this word comes from a Latin term meaning "other," and that's the altruist's concern—other people. While selfish people like the egotist make sure they look out for number one, the altruist is unselfish, putting the welfare of others ahead of self-interest. The adjective form is **altruistic**.

- *Bill may be very rich, but he sure is **altruistic**, devoting so much time and money to making the world a better place.*

- *The golden rule, according to the **altruist**, is true.*

2. Misanthrope (MISS-an-thrope)

Some nouns describe haters of males or of females, but this one is not gender-specific. Anyone can be disliked by a misanthrope, "one who hates or mistrusts humankind."

- *Julian had turned into such a **misanthrope** that he could not stand to speak to people, let alone see them, and so he spent most of his days locked up in his room.*

- *Only a **misanthrope** would believe that no one would be willing to donate money to the tsunami relief fund.*

3. Recluse (REK-kloos or re-KLOOS)

Recluses are people who choose to live in solitude as much as possible. The root word in Latin means "closed in." *Hermit* would be a good synonym, whereas its root **eremite** is a fancy word used mostly for one who withdraws from the world for religious reasons.

- *Probably the best-known **recluse** in twentieth-century literature is Arthur "Boo" Radley of* To Kill a Mockingbird. *He emerges from his house only in an unusual situation, saving a child from the murderous attack of the evil Bob Ewell.*

- *Milton's poem* Paradise Regained *refers to the Biblical John the Baptist as a "glorious **eremite**."*

4. Troglodyte (TROG-luh-dite)

The literal meaning (from the Greek) is "cave dweller," but as commonly used today, *troglodyte* means "a real loner," or "a person of crude, brutal character."

- *That "nice young man" you fixed me up with turned out to be a complete **troglodyte**.*

- *You've never heard of these musicians and artists? What, have you been living in a cave, like a **troglodyte**?*

5. Ascetic (uh-SET-ick)

Maybe this person doesn't hide out in caves, but he does deny himself many of life's luxuries. Ascetics live an austere, simple life, perhaps for religious reasons, and abstain from most worldly pleasures.

- *He won't have a beer with us, much less go out partying—what an **ascetic**.*

- *The **ascetic** life's not for her; she thinks life's too short to miss out on life's pleasures.*

Milton's poem Paradise Regained *refers to the Biblical John the Baptist as a "glorious **eremite**."*

6. Voluptuary (vul-UP-choo-air-ee)

If the ascetic is at one end of the pleasure path, the voluptuary is at the opposite end. Far from shunning pleasure, the voluptuary seeks it, and may even make it the primary goal of life.

- *He's a true **voluptuary**—wine, women, and song— plus the best in food, clothing, art, and music. He wants it all, all the time.*

- *Did she really get herself to a nunnery? What a surprise—she used to be such a thoroughgoing **voluptuary**.*

7. Stoic (STOW-ik)

Swinging the pendulum back toward the lower end of the excitement scale, we find the stoic—a person who is (or at least tries to be) indifferent to both life's pleasures and its pain. Originally designating a member of an ancient Greek school of philosophy (**stoicism**), the term now applies to anyone who is seemingly indifferent to passions, especially to someone who bears up well under the stresses of life.

- *He has suffered one tragedy after another, but maintained his **stoicism** through it all.*

- *Don't be such a **stoic**—go ahead and have a good cry.*

8. Curmudgeon (ker-MUDGE-un)

This bad guy is a grouch, a grump. He (or she) is in a perpetually bad mood. Weirdly enough, no one seems to know the origin of this unique noun that suggests a growling cur.

- *If Bobbie Sue doesn't lose some of her **curmudgeonly** ways, she will find herself without any friends or professional allies.*

- *Before his conversion to kindness, Dickens's Ebenezer Scrooge was the embodiment of a **curmudgeon**— and stingy to boot.*

9. Skeptic (SKEP-tik)

The identifying quality of the skeptic is doubt— unwillingness to accept much of anything on face value. Like *stoic*, this term comes from an ancient Greek philosophy—**skepticism**. (A cynic is even more—well, cynical. While the skeptic doubts, the cynic curmudgeonly disbelieves.)

- *There are true believers—people who swallow political or religions beliefs whole—and then there are **skeptics**—people who accept nothing without careful and thorough examination.*

- *Don't be such a **skeptic**—why would I lie to you?*

10. Pollyanna (POL-lee-AN-na)

The original Pollyanna was a fictional character who found some reason for joy in any situation. Now the term often has negative connotations, commonly referring to someone who's foolishly and blindly optimistic. It is usually capitalized, and the adjective form is **Pollyannaish.**

- *The old curmudgeon thought anyone who believed in the chance of world peace in our lifetimes was being pathologically **Pollyannaish**.*

- *But his wife saw at least a little good in everyone and everything—she was a **Pollyanna** in the best sense of the word.*

20 olio

Here's the penultimate mixed-bag chapter. An olio is a collection of different things. For example, a band could perform a musical olio—a variety of songs in different styles.

1. Tawdry (TAW-dree)

This adjective describes something literally cheap or gaudy in appearance, or something more figuratively shameful. It enshrines St. Audrey (think sain-TAW-dree), a seventh-century English saint whose name was given to a fair that sold decorative items such as lace. Alas for St. Audrey, the word degenerated into a completely negative meaning.

- *At twelve, Jenny attempted to acquire glamour by using all her mother's cosmetics but achieved only an unappealing, **tawdry** look.*

- *Why is it that some people enjoy revealing their **tawdry** secrets to a nationwide television audience?*

2. Specter (rhymes with *Hector*)

Literally meaning "a ghost" (or wraith or apparition), this noun is now often used for any disturbing image of a future disturbance.

- *On the night before the battle in which he was killed, Richard III was visited by **specters** of all those whom he had murdered, at least in Shakespeare's version of his life.*

- *The **specter** of a lifetime of minimum wage jobs kept Lenore motivated to continue prepping to pass the bar exam.*

3. Caveat (KAV-ee-at)

A caveat is a warning, a caution. Interestingly, it comes directly from use in a Latin phrase that is still used in English: *Caveat emptor*—let the buyer beware (for he knows not what he buys).

- *"This medicine can be very effective," said Dr. Charlatan. "Just one **caveat**: never take it with pomegranate juice."*

- *Cindy knew the banker was just trying to be super cautious, but her enthusiasm over the loan for her new business declined as she listened to **caveat** after **caveat** about on-time repayment.*

4. Vitiate (VISH-ee-ate)

In its harshest usage, this verb can refer to the process of corrupting someone's morals, but it's usually employed in the milder sense of lessening the quality of something, making something ineffective.

- *"Don't put all that pepper in the soup," cried the chef to his assistant. "You're going to **vitiate** my vichyssoise!"*

- *Russell was a perfectionist: his staff had to constantly remind him that the project would not be **vitiated** just because one tiny detail was not to his liking.*

5. Expatiate (ex-PAY-she-ate)

If you expatiate on a topic, you expand your thoughts; you speak or write at length. (Memory hook: think of the word *spatial*.)

- *Those who **expatiate** on the details of a dream they had during the previous night are highly likely to bore their luncheon partners.*

- *"I knew Malcolm was the man for me," said Mindy, "when he allowed me to **expatiate** on my memories of my childhood without once interrupting with memories of his own."*

*The German philosopher Friedrich Nietzsche once said, "The most dangerous physicians are those born actors who imitate born physicians with a perfectly deceptive **guile**."*

6. Guile (rhymes with *style*)

This noun means "skillful cunning" or "deceit" and comes from the Old English word for "sorcery." **Beguile**, a related verb, comes a bit closer to the word's original roots; though it also means "to deceive," it often suggests a kind of cunning that is more charming than treacherous.

- *The German philosopher Friedrich Nietzsche once said, "The most dangerous physicians are those born actors who imitate born physicians with a perfectly deceptive **guile**."*

- *Caught taking an extra cupcake off the food line in the cafeteria, Rasheen **beguiled** the server with a bright smile and a shrug and said, "It's for my friend who forgot to take one when she picked up her lunch."*

7. Askance (uh-SKANCE)

This adverb is nearly always used with some form of the verb *look,* and describes a look that is mistrustful or disapproving. It is of unknown origin.

- *When the White House Chief of Staff stated that the President would probably look **askance** at the issue, was that code for saying that there would be a veto?*

- *Shakespeare made a verb of this adverb and referred to those who would "askaunce their eyes"; the public, however, must have looked **askance** at this usage, for it never caught on.*

8. Cloying (KLOY-ing)

This adjective originally comes from the Latin meaning "to drive a nail into." It's no wonder it means something that is so overly sweet and rich that it tastes bad. It can be used literally or figuratively.

- *Allison loves her boyfriend, but she is overwhelmed by his **cloying** expressions of fidelity.*

- *I only put lemon in my tea because I find the taste of honey too **cloying**.*

9. Debacle (de-BAK-al or DEB-a-kul)

This noun is slightly different from *travesty* although the consequences are the same. There is no element of mockery here; it means "a sudden, disastrous downfall" or "defeat."

- *After the **debacle** at Gettysburg, the Confederate army never again crossed the Mason-Dixon Line.*

- *In 1943, the German army in Russia was trapped in a hopeless **debacle** of its own making.*

10. Winnow (WIN-oh)

From the Old English word for "wind," this verb once meant literally "to separate the grain from the chaff" by means of a current of air. It has since come to have a more figurative meaning—"to rid of undesirable parts" or "to separate the good from the bad."

- *After weeks of rigorous interviews, the list was **winnowed** down to the three most-experienced job candidates.*

- *"I have finally **winnowed** my book down from three thousand pages to one thousand pages," said Fabienne. "Maybe now I can get a publisher to read it before rejecting it."*

Quiz #4

CATEGORY A

Match each definition on the right with the appropriate word in the column on the left.

_____ veracity   A. a cave-dweller, loner

_____ parsimonious   B. pertaining to budgetary matters

_____ canard   C. overly frugal, stingy

_____ troglodyte   D. honesty, truthfulness

_____ fiscal   E. a damaging lie

CATEGORY B

Select a word from the list below that best fits each of the sentences on the next page. (One sentence calls for two words.) Some words won't be used at all.

penurious	lucrative
circumlocution	pariah
husbandry	cloying
voluptuary	ostracize

1. The politician hardly ever gave a direct answer; his responses were marked by repeated _____.

2. She was glad to be a teacher, even though it wasn't the most _____ job she could have taken.

3. He loved the finer things in life: fine food, fine wine, fine music—he was a true _____.

4. When they discovered the cult leader's secret and sordid life, everyone decided to _____ him; he became a veritable _____.

5. Both the dessert and the overly sentimental tale were _____.

CATEGORY C

1. He became an ascetic, living the life of a mendicant. What was his life like, and what was the source of his income?

2. You ask what their attitude is toward others? Well, he's a misanthrope; she's an altruist. Explain.

3. She was somewhat skeptical of his motives; she felt that many of his remarks were double entendres. Explain.

4. I'm no sadist, but when I saw the officer giving the rude driver a ticket, I had a strong feeling of schadenfreude. Explain.

5. He looked askance at her when he learned that she was affluent, yet parsimonious. Explain.

21
praise or blame?

Lots of written and spoken words are spent in praising and blaming others, perhaps not enough of the former and too much of the latter. Here are a few words about both praise and blame.

1. **Ovation** (oh-VAY-shun)

As used these days, an ovation usually means "applause for a public performance"—especially enthusiastic, prolonged applause. To ancient Romans, the word meant a victory celebration (although a second-rate one, just below a triumph).

- *Not only did they applaud her lecture on the importance of vocabulary building, they even gave her a standing* **ovation**.

- *One guitar company calls its instrument an* **Ovation**—*perhaps to entice wannabe stars.*

2. **Adulation** (ad-you-LAY-shun)

This word comes from the Latin root meaning "to flatter." But as used today, it's a bit stronger. To adulate means "to admire strongly"—so strongly, in fact, that the word suggests excessive, even servile admiration.

- *The fan's **adulation** for Derek Jeter was so great that he changed his own name to Derek.*

- *The students felt nothing but **adulation** for their history teacher until they found out that he belonged to an illegal extremist group.*

3. Vilify (VIL-if-eye)

This verb means "to bad-mouth, to speak ill of." Or, as the sound of the word suggests, "to portray as a villain." The noun form is **vilification**.

- *His constant **vilification** of his political opponents was so extreme that it eventually had a boomerang effect, turning voters away.*

- *He didn't use many facts, and was unable to support his statements. His motto seemed to be "Don't bother to verify, just **vilify**."*

4. Castigate (CAST-ih-gate)

From the Latin word for "pure," this verb means "to harshly scold, criticize severely," or "to punish." Other words from the same root include *chastise,* which means "to punish by beating" or "harshly criticize," and *chasten,* which means to "correct by punishment" or "verbally subdue."

- *In her letter to the urban planning department, Katya used all of the harsh language she had learned in law school to **castigate** city officials for failing to supervise the proper installation of wheelchair ramps in most of the apartment buildings on her block.*

- *With her voice raised in anger and her finger wagging with fierce disapproval, Martha **castigated** her boyfriend for having yet again forgotten their anniversary.*

5. Encomium (en-CO-me-um)

An encomium is a warm expression of high praise, often an official one, part of a ceremony.

- *The returning victor was given an **encomium** by the queen herself.*

- *At her retirement ceremony, she heard **encomiums** from inside and outside the organization.*

*Simon's brutality as a talent show judge was so severe that contestants would often burst into tears as he **excoriated** them for the mistakes they had made during their performances.*

6. Excoriate (ex-CORE-ee-ate)

From the Latin word that means "to take off the skin," this verb means not only literally "to remove the skin," but also to censure strongly, as if flaying with words.

- *Simon's brutality as a talent show judge was so severe that contestants would often burst into tears as he excoriated* them for the mistakes they had made during their performances.

- When Mara fell from her bike, her ankle was cut and her knee was **excoriated**.

7. Malign (muh-LINE)

The *mal-* gives us a clue, because it means "bad, evil." And the person who maligns another is saying things that are not only intended to damage a reputation, but that are generally untrue. (Malign can also simply mean "evil," as a malign influence or person.)

- He's utterly without character, and will **malign** anyone who opposes him.

- The gloomy weather and disappointing financial news had a **malign** influence on his mood.

8. Accolade (AK-ka-laid)

The *col* in this word comes from the Latin term for "neck," and this noun originally meant a hug or embrace given when dubbing a new knight. Today it can mean any form of praise or acknowledgement, although it often suggests a somewhat formal recognition.

- The liner notes listed many **accolades** from stars.

- The reviewers gave her **accolades** for her new book about interesting words.

9. Eulogy (YOU-luh-gee)

A eulogy is another form of praise. It's almost always used to mean a speech or written work in praise of a deceased person—often a speech delivered at a memorial service.

- *The ostensible **eulogy** contained a good deal of self-praise for the person delivering it.*

- *You can learn anything from computers—here's a pop-up promising to help you write a **eulogy**.*

10. Libel (LIE-b'l) and Slander (SLAN-der)

To slander is to tell untrue and damaging stories about someone. To libel is to do much the same, but in writing. (Slander can be a punishable crime, as can libel—which is written slander.) The adjectives are **libelous** and **slanderous**, respectively.

- *Sirrah, that's a **slanderous** accusation, and I'll not stand for it.*

- *After the paper published the harshly critical column, she considered suing for **libel**.*

22 short words

Some short words can be at least as interesting, and as useful, as long ones. These three-letter words are good examples of little words that can make a big difference in your vocabulary.

1. Fey (fay)

We all know someone who's just a little different, maybe, or (to use a couple more shorties) a little odd or off, but often in an interesting way.

- *His parents didn't know what to make of the oddly dressed and disconcertingly frank young woman. They liked her, but considered her a bit fey.*

- *She kept snakes as pets, read occult books, and did other things most people would consider a little fey.*

2. Coy (rhymes with boy)

This word describes someone—usually a woman or girl—who's something of a tease, someone who might playfully give indirect answers, often in a flirting way.

- *When asked if she had a date for the prom, she lowered her eyes, smiled **coyly,** and said she was still considering her many offers.*

- *Her **coy** ways irritated some of the girls, but enticed the boys.*

3. Erg (urg)

Whether used as a separate word (meaning a unit of work) or as a building block for longer terms, this word serves us well. **Ergonomics** is the study of the way things and people work. You might call a lazy friend an **ergophobe**, or refer to a workaholic as an **ergomaniac**.

- ***Ergonomic** studies helped improve the time and effort needed to assemble the products.*

- *The chiropractor said I should try an **ergonomically** designed chair to reduce strain while I worked.*

4. Cud (rhymes with *mud*)

This word is probably used more often in a figurative sense than a literal one. Some animals (cows, deer, etc.) have multiple stomachs, and sort of burp back up partially digested nuggets of food for further chewing. Such a nugget is called a cud (or rumen).

- *The vacant-eyed, gum-chewing young man reminded me of a cow chewing its **cud**.*

- *Don't just sit there chewing your **cud**—let's go do something exciting.*

5. Yen (rhymes with *hen*)

A yen is a desire, often (but not always) a sexual or physical one.

- *The other girls thought her a bit boy-crazy, saying she had a **yen** for men.*

- *All this word study makes me hungry; I have a **yen** for a big, juicy steak.*

> *Although Lynette had never studied Italian, she could **eke** out the meaning of a newspaper article in a Roman newspaper through her understanding of Latin and French.*

6. Ilk (rhymes with *milk*)

This term means "kind" (in the sense of category) or "sort." Although it can be used in a neutral sense (as in a scientific grouping), it often carries a negative connotation, so use it carefully to avoid unintentionally offending someone.

- *The potato bug and its **ilk** did a lot of damage to the crops.*

- *He and his **ilk** are stirring up a lot of trouble; I wish they'd go away.*

7. Eke (eek)

As a verb, *eke* carries two senses: the older one expresses the idea of "adding to" or "increasing," while the one more in use today carries the sense of "managing, but with difficulty." (Extra trivia for word lovers: our word *nickname* was originally *an eke-name*, an "additional" name. The *n* of *an* moved over and became part of the next word. *Umpire* went the other way: it was originally *a numpere*.)

- *Mr. Compton **eked** out a living as a teacher by continuing to work on the family farm in the summers.*

- *Although Lynette had never studied Italian, she could **eke** out the meaning of a newspaper article in a Roman newspaper through her understanding of Latin and French.*

8. Ken (rhymes with *hen*)

This word means "understanding, mental comprehension." It's often used in the negative, as in "beyond someone's ken."

- *I studied hard on integral calculus, but found it beyond my **ken**.*

- *Barbie, with a little help from her boyfriend, found it well within her **ken**.*

9. Wan (rhymes with *Don*)

Usually found in company with *pale,* this word describes someone (in literature, usually a delicate young woman) who's fair of skin and weakened or frightened by something.

- *The folk song described the girl as so pale and **wan** that she looked likely to faint.*

- *You look so **wan** and washed out—you really need to get some sun and outdoor exercise.*

10. Jot (rhymes with *not*)

We know this as a verb, meaning to quickly write something down (maybe a phone number). But it's also used as a noun—from a variant spelling of *iota*, the smallest letter in the Greek alphabet—meaning something very small, maybe insignificant. We often hear it alongside its twin, **tittle**, which is even smaller—it's a dot or other small mark in printing.

- *What a troglodyte—he cares not a **jot** what's going on in the outside world.*

- *She wouldn't give a **jot** or a **tittle** for all the romance novels in the States—she reads nothing but classics.*

23
the time of your life

We're all concerned about time—whether we're wasting it, worrying about not having enough of it, or trying to manage it. These words reflect that concern.

1. **Synchronicity** (sin-cruh-NIS-sat-ee)

This noun means "occurring at the same time," but to some people it carries the idea that maybe things happen at the same time because they're guided by a higher, unknown force. The verb form is **synchronize**.

- *Historians of science have found amazing incidences of **synchronicity**, when similar major discoveries have occurred simultaneously on different continents without communication between the researchers.*

- *Although he said he had just happened to be going for a walk at the same time, she doubted that the **synchronicity** was accidental.*

2. **Diurnal** (dye-UR-nal)

This adjective means "occurring in a twenty-four-hour period" or "daily" or "occurring or active in the daytime, rather than at night." It comes from the Latin word for "day."

- *Norman's **diurnal** routine included a two-hour weight-lifting session at the gym, a five-mile run, and one hundred sit-ups, but still he was overweight. "It must be all those cream puffs I eat," he sighed, looking down at the scale.*

- *Many poets, such as William Wordsworth, have written about earth's "**diurnal** course" to describe the passage of a day.*

3. Nocturnal (nok-TUR-nal)

From the Latin word for "night," this adjective means "occurring at night" or "most active at night." A related word is **nocturne**, which is a painting of a night scene or a piece of music with a pensive, dreamy mood.

- *A **nocturnal** creature, my cat Bruiser wanders around the neighborhood at night, searching through trash cans for food and getting into fights with the neighbors' pets.*

- *Most pianists aspire to play Chopin's pensive but difficult piano **nocturnes**.*

4. Horology (hor-OL-la-gee)

People have long been fascinated with ways to measure time. Horology is the art and science of making clocks and other time-measuring instruments, as practiced by **horologists**.

- *Although Chris was proud of his work on clocks, he disliked being introduced as a **horologist**.*

- *Early **horologists** used dripping water and other imprecise tools in their efforts to measure time.*

5. Sidereal (side-EER-ee-ul)

One of the first ways time was measured was by the stars—including our sun. This adjective means "determined by or from the stars."

- *Adrift at sea, he estimated the passage of the night by the changing **sidereal** configuration.*

- *Time has long been reckoned by **sidereal** observation.*

*Many poets, such as William Wordsworth, have written about earth's "**diurnal** course" to describe the passage of a day.*

6. Crepuscular (crep-US-cue-lur)

This adjective means "dim" or "like twilight." It is used mainly to describe the quality of physical light.

- *Having only one small window, the basement was damp and **crepuscular**, even on a bright summer morning.*

- *More car accidents occur at dusk than at any other time of day, because it is more difficult to judge distances or see other drivers in **crepuscular** light.*

7. Anachronism (an-AK-kron-ism)

This is a noun for the fairly common literary technique of representing someone or something as existing in other than chronological or historical order. So, for instance, a play that includes a scene in which Sigmund Freud has a dinner conversation with William Shakespeare relies on anachronism to make a point. The adjective form is **anachronistic**.

- *Iago's horn-rimmed eyeglasses were an **anachronism** that marred the student production of* Othello *currently being performed at P.S. 119.*

- *The story was set in the present time, but included such **anachronistic** features as time travel and cavemen.*

8. Sempiternal (sem-puh-TUR-nul)

Eternal often means "existing forever," without beginning or end. Something that's sempiternal has a beginning, but no end. Once begun, it is of never-ending duration.

- *As a child, she grappled with the concept of how anything could be **sempiternal**—how it could go on forever.*

- *Many sagacious grown-ups are **sempiternally** grappling with the same problem, trying to wrap their minds around the inexplicable idea of anything without end.*

9. Precedent (PRESS-uh-dent)

Precede means "to go before," and a precedent is something that happened before, and that influences what happens later. It's often used in a legal sense, because judges consider earlier rulings (case law) in arriving at a decision.

- *She said she'd approve my request this once, but not to consider it a **precedent** for future actions.*

- *Supreme Court rulings are powerful not just in the immediate case, but as long-lasting and influential **precedents**.*

10. Procrastinate (pro-CRASS-tuh-nate)

This word means "to put off, delay." (We meant to list this word earlier, but didn't get around to it.) Someone who procrastinates is a **procrastinator**.

- *He can't seem to get his homework done until the last minute—he's such a **procrastinator**.*

- *It's okay to look before you leap, but don't take so long a look that you **procrastinate** in doing what needs to be done.*

24 travel words

From Jack Kerouac's famous novel *On the Road* to Willie Nelson's immortal song "On the Road Again," there's no dearth of sentiments—or words—about travel.

1. Odyssey (ODD-is-ee)

This useful noun for a long trip comes straight from that great traveler Odysseus, hero of Homer's *Odyssey*. Today it can describe a literal journey or a journey of the intellect or spirit.

- *My grandparents took a world cruise to celebrate their golden wedding anniversary. What an **odyssey**! They sailed all the way around the world, with stops in ports on every continent.*

- *Lex felt he had undergone quite an **odyssey** in his first two years of college, for he had changed his career goals as well as his philosophical outlook on life.*

2. Gad (rhymes with *bad*)

As a verb, it's often mildly critical. It means "to move about, travel," usually in a kind of aimless way. It's not related to the old-fashioned expression "Ye gads!"

- *Ashley has been **gadding** all over the country, trying to decide what colleges she wants to apply to.*

- ***Gadding** about to different malls to compare sneaker prices can waste a lot of time and gas money.*

3. Veer (rhymes with *clear*)

This verb describes a sharp swerving, moving abruptly from one side or the other.

- *The taxi driver's skill allowed him to **veer** quickly off the road when the impromptu neighborhood poodle parade came into his lane.*

- *"My political views are confused," moaned Mona. "Sometimes I sympathize with the conservative point of view, but then a news story may cause me to **veer** over to the far left."*

4. Interloper (IN-ter-LOPE-er)

Interlopers are people (or plants!) who enter a region where they are not welcome.

- *Saki's great short story "The **Interlopers**" involves feuding relatives who are forced to confront a very special kind of intruder.*

- *Bruce and Patrice's attempt to maintain a garden of English perennials required them to spend hours each month rooting out the native loosestrife, a persistent **interloper** among the cowslips and columbine.*

5. **Sojourn** (SO-jurn)

From the Latin for "to spend the day," this noun means "temporary stay" or "brief period of residence." It may also be used as a verb.

- *Last summer, the Sugarmans rented a villa overlooking a vineyard in central Tuscany, and made regular **sojourns** to the surrounding hill towns of Montepulciano, Montalcino, Assisi, and Volterra.*

- *On their honeymoon, the Lesters **sojourned** to San Sebastian, Spain, before traveling to the French Riviera.*

Henry Fielding's 1749 novel Tom Jones *is a wonderful example of the on-the-road novel. Fielding delightfully punctuates the hero's **picaresque** adventures with a preface to each of the eighteen sections.*

6. **Peregrination** (PEH-reg-grin-AY-shun)

This noun comes from the Latin word for "foreigner" and means "to wander or travel abroad." The verb form is **peregrinate**.

- *After her sophomore year in college, Kamisha planned a year of **peregrination**, starting in Africa and then traveling to Latin America and the Far East.*

- *Giving in to his wanderlust, Damian quit his job at One Hour Photo to **peregrinate** through Europe; he left Boston for Paris with an open-return ticket and no hotel reservations.*

7. Cicerone (SIS-eh-RONE-ee or CHI-che-RONE-eh)

We've borrowed this word that means "guide for sightseers" straight from the Italian. It originally refers to Marcus Tullius Cicero (106–43 BC), the famous Roman orator, statesman, and philosopher. You're more likely to see it in classic literature than to hear it commonly used today.

- *It will be terrific to have Julie as our **cicerone** when David and I visit Florence in April, since she's lived there for two years and really knows her way around the city.*

- *It is impossible to visit the famous temples of Angkor Wat in Cambodia without a **cicerone**, as the ruins need to be protected from plundering by thieves and vandals.*

8. Transcend (trans-SEND)

This verb, which means "to go beyond the limits of something," always refers to travel of a nonliteral variety.

- *Sarah Lee and Charlie hope to **transcend** their past disagreements and enter a new era of good feeling.*

- *Howie's interest in marine life may **transcend** the boundaries of normal: he has a room in his small house devoted to shelves and tubs overflowing with cowries, conches, sand dollars, and shells of sea turtles.*

9. Vagrant (VAY-grint)

This noun means "one who wanders from place to place without a permanent home or means of livelihood." It can also be used as an adjective. A more contemporary term, also used as a noun or an adjective, is *homeless.*

- *Since the Depression, many **vagrants** in Manhattan have built temporary shelters beneath the highway overpass leading to the Brooklyn Bridge.*

- *Despite the sign reading "No **Vagrants**" on the door of the public restrooms, a homeless man was found sleeping on the tile floor beneath the sinks.*

10. Picaresque (pick-a-RESK or peek-a-RESK)

This adjective comes into English from Spanish, where a *picaro* is a rogue, a rascal. In English, a picaresque novel is one where a main character of low economic status, usually a male, takes to the road and lives by his wits in a loosely-connected series of adventures.

- *Henry Fielding's 1749 novel Tom Jones is a wonderful example of the on-the-road novel. Fielding delightfully punctuates the hero's **picaresque** adventures with a preface to each of the eighteen sections.*

- *Jamie hoped to impress his English teacher when he wrote that Mark Twain's Adventures of Huckleberry Finn was "a rare example of a **picaresque** bildungs-roman" (a novel about growing up).*

25 potpourri

A potpourri (pope-uh-REE) is a mixture of unrelated objects, and that's what you have here—words with little in common except that they're interesting and useful, helpful in expanding your vocabulary.

1. Elliptical (ee-LIP-tik-ul)

This adjective is often used to describe speech or writing where some words have been left out, either intentionally or by error. The origin is from the Greek for "falls short of"—just as the mathematical **ellipse** falls short of being a circle.

- *If you shout, "Help!" you have uttered an **elliptical** sentence; you did not need to say, "I need help!"*

- *A major difference between poetry of the late nineteenth century and that of the late twentieth century is that the latter is much more **elliptical**. The reader must often supply the implied connection between two lines or passages.*

2. Evanescent (ev-un-ESS-unt)

This adjective is from the Latin term literally meaning "to vanish," but you can use it figuratively as well—for anything that is very short-lived, barely discernible, or ephemeral. The noun form is **evanescence**.

- *They dreamed of becoming famous novelists; their dreams proved **evanescent**.*

- *But their disappointment was also a matter of **evanescence**, for they soon found happiness writing vocabulary books.*

3. Sedulous (SED-u-lus)

This adjective describes hard work, consistently applied to the task at hand. It originates in two Latin words meaning "without trickery," a fact that shows the sedulous person isn't trying to take any short cuts!

- *Josh's high grades are due to a combination of natural intelligence and **sedulous** effort.*

- *The poet W. B. Yeats **sedulously** sought beautiful images to use in his writing, and was delighted when his new wife indicated help was available from the realm of the supernatural.*

4. Effulgent (ef-ULL-junt)

A good word when you need to describe a radiant sunset or a splendid display of luminescence, it means "brightly shining, diffusing a flood of light." The noun form is **effulgence**.

- *The sudden sunrise cast a broad path of **effulgent** light across the lake's surface.*

- *The **effulgence** of the Milky Way as seen from the mountaintop is a treat to savor.*

5. Pandemic (pan-DEM-ik)

Yes, it sounds a lot like *epidemic*. Just as that word means a spreading of a disease, pandemic suggests an even wider spread of the contagion. *Pan* comes from Greek meaning "all." Like epidemic, it can be used figuratively.

- *Today we don't regard "flu" as a very serious condition, but **pandemic** influenza in the early twentieth century was fatal to a large number of people.*

- *"If the unemployment epidemic in this country is not to become a **pandemic**, we must act now to decrease the number of jobs being outsourced to other countries," said Dr. Mehta, who had made an extensive study of the situation.*

***Bucolic** poetry has a long tradition, for both Greek and Roman poets depict shepherds philosophically discussing life, love, and art—everything but the care of sheep.*

6. Exonerate (eg-ZAHN-er-ate)

The root words have the idea of "laying down a burden." And, indeed, if you are exonerated, you are freed from a responsibility or blame, whether in a legal matter or something less official.

- *Graham was accused of being the "redheaded boy" who threw an egg out the second floor of the school building onto a passerby in the street below, but he* **exonerated** *himself by having every student in his calculus class affirm that he was in a first-floor classroom at the time.*

- *"No officer worth his salt," said Major Rigsby-Radnor, "would want to be* **exonerated** *from his duty of fighting for Her Majesty Queen Griselda; in fact, I insist on leading the charge."*

7. Bucolic (bew-KOLL-ik)

This adjective meaning "typical of the countryside" always has a connotation suggestive of leafy peace and quiet. Appropriately enough, the root is the Greek word for "cow."

- *Selina likes the combination of rural and urban: when in a city, she seeks out* **bucolic** *pockets such as small parks with trees and fountains, and in the country she can be found buying bandanas in the general store.*

- **Bucolic** *poetry has a long tradition, for both Greek and Roman poets depict shepherds philosophically discussing life, love, and art—everything but the care of sheep.*

8. Coalesce (co-uh-LESS)

Applied to physical things, this verb means "to merge, come together, fuse." It's also useful when you want to describe nonphysical things that blend or merge into unity.

- *The ingredients coalesced into a sumptuous batter.*

- *After repeated practice sessions, the sounds of the recently formed band finally coalesced into the sweet music the director had been hearing in his head all along.*

9. Biodiversity (BY-o-die-VERSE-it-ee)

This word is not too hard to figure out—*bio* means life—so we're talking about the diversity of life, the number and variety of living things—plants and animals—in a given area (or in the whole world, to take the broad view). We're including the word because scientists are now recognizing the profound importance of maintaining different species, and the possibly catastrophic effects of letting too many species become extinct—as is happening when rain forests are being clear-cut, killing almost all the plants and animals living there.

- *Charles Darwin saw the importance of biodiversity long before most scientists had begun to give it serious thought.*

- *Perhaps the leading advocate of biodiversity today is the eminent biologist Edward O. Wilson, winner of two Pulitzer Prizes, who said that destroying a rain forest for economic gain is like burning a Renaissance painting to cook a meal.*

10. Glissando (gluh-SON-doh)

A musical term that you can apply to other types of sound, *glissando* is from the French word for "slide." And that bit of etymology will help you remember what it means, because the slide trombone is the premier instrument for producing glissandos. (They can be produced on other instruments, including the piano.)

- *I love circus music, with all those delicious **glissando** sounds from the trombones.*

- *The freight train roared by the platform, its whistle ripping a **glissando** out into the night as it passed.*

Quiz #5

CATEGORY A

Match each definition on the right with the appropriate word in the column on the left.

_____ accolades   A. a longing, a strong desire

_____ procrastinate   B. to go beyond

_____ transcend   C. to delay unnecessarily

_____ vilify   D. words of praise

_____ yen   E. to describe as worse than the reality

CATEGORY B

Select a word from the list below that best fits each of the sentences on the next page. Some words won't be used at all.

accolade	coalesce
coy	crepuscular
effulgent	exonerate
fey	gad
pandemic	wan

1. Everyone is wondering if the jury's verdict will _____ the man who so ardently maintains his innocence.

2. The guy we offered the job to should either accept or decline. He needs to stop being so _____ about the matter.

3. The speaker was interesting, but the trained dogs received the Vox Populi award, the highest _____ from the crowd.

4. His _____ appearance made us wonder if he was feeling under the weather.

5. The _____ atmosphere of the close of day has been poetically termed "the violet hour."

CATEGORY C

1. You believe your cicerone deserves accolades. What's the situation?

2. You're sedulous about attempting to bring horology within your ken. What's going on?

3. If you had to castigate an interloper, what would you be doing?

4. That picaresque novel has a lot of anachronisms in it. Explain.

5. His interest in bucolic poetry was evanescent. Explain.

appendix: quiz answers

Quiz #1

CATEGORY A

C

D

E

B

A

CATEGORY B

1. placate

2. vacillate

3. pique, clandestine

4. harbinger

5. extant

CATEGORY C

1. He expected the speech to electrify them, to shock them into immediate action. They found his talk uninspiring, even boring.

2. It means that Ann's interest lasted only a very short time.

3. She might frequently change her mind, her clothing, and her social calendar, but she probably wouldn't drop out of her senior year to go bicycling around Europe.

4. He meant that the responsibility that came with his position did not extend to frequent and close friendship with common people.

5. It made the scolding unnecessary, no longer needed.

Quiz #2

CATEGORY A

D

A

E

C

B

CATEGORY B

1. germane

2. eclectic

3. quintessence

4. innuendo

5. chimera

CATEGORY C

1. Since a pyrrhic victory is one where the losses outweigh the technical triumph, you'd be unlikely to feel a sense of restorative cleansing that a catharsis should bring.

2. A kakistocracy is rule by the worst, so you'd probably feel gloomy a lot of the time—unless you yourself were one of the worst people in the society.

3. You might be happy about a pristine or very clean new copy of Shakespeare, but unless you wanted something for very young children, you probably wouldn't want the bowdlerized version, one that makes Shakespeare's language completely G-rated.

4. Tough choice here: do you find it easier to be around a friend in a gloomy frame of mind or one who's really angry?

5. Since a plutocracy is a society ruled by the wealthiest, light joking conversation about it would probably, at best, be some kind of parlor game, an exercise of wit to find reason why you, say, love having people buy their way into office.

Quiz #3

CATEGORY A

B

C

E

A

D

CATEGORY B

1. feral

2. ebullient

3. protégé, mentor

4. euphoric

5. cryptic

CATEGORY C

1. The judge meant that the prisoners should be pardoned; they were almost certainly grateful.

2. The home would most likely be filled with kittens; gravid means pregnant. (Did you know that an *ailurophile* is a cat-lover?)

3. She probably enjoyed life immensely, as joie de vivre means "joy of life." But she was probably at least somewhat moderate, because a hedonist is one who makes life's pleasures the number-one goal.

4. *Inauspicious* means "not looking all that great for the future," so the spat may have put the wedding plans (nuptials) in doubt.

5. An avuncular person (literally "like an uncle") is kind, guiding, helpful; the way he dealt with the students helped them develop a feeling of team spirit.

Quiz #4

CATEGORY A

D

C

E

A

B

CATEGORY B

1. circumlocution

2. lucrative

3. voluptuary

4. ostracize, pariah

5. cloying

CATEGORY C

1. His life was simple, devoid of all luxuries, free of frivolity. Begging was the source of his income.

2. He hates everybody; she loves everybody (or at least is inclined to be good to others).

3. She had serious doubts about his true goals, because many of his remarks seemed to have double meanings— often with sexual overtones.

4. I don't like to see or inflict pain, but it gave me a feeling of deep satisfaction to see the rude driver get his comeuppance.

5. He gave her a doubtful, questioning look on learning that she was wealthy, yet stingy.

Quiz #5

CATEGORY A

D

C

B

E

A

CATEGORY B

1. exonerate

2. coy

3. accolade

4. wan

5. crepuscular

CATEGORY C

1. You want to give high praise to your super-excellent tour guide.

2. You're working hard to bring knowledge of clocks into your sphere of learning.

3. "Get out of here! You don't belong here!" You're scolding someone or something—maybe a troop of mice—that has entered a place where he, she, or it doesn't belong.

4. This novel about adventures of an on-the-road main character must be clumsily written about an earlier period, because it has anachronisms such as having a traveler on a donkey sending a text message.

5. His fondness for poems about lowing cows and grazing sheep didn't last, so his temporary passion for nature poetry should be called evanescent.

about the authors

Edward B. Fiske served for seventeen years as education editor of the *New York Times*, and he is the author of *Fiske Guide to Colleges* and numerous other books on college admissions. Jane Mallison has taught for more than twenty years and has served on the College Board SAT Committee. David Hatcher has written and co-written several books, workbooks, and other training materials on vocabulary, writing, proofreading and editing, and related subjects. His writing has been published in the *Washington Post* and in national magazines. Jane Mallison and David Hatcher have MA degrees from, respectively, Duke University and Indiana University. This is their first collaboration since their joint journalistic efforts as undergraduates.